Res<u>t</u>oring the Vision of the End-times Church

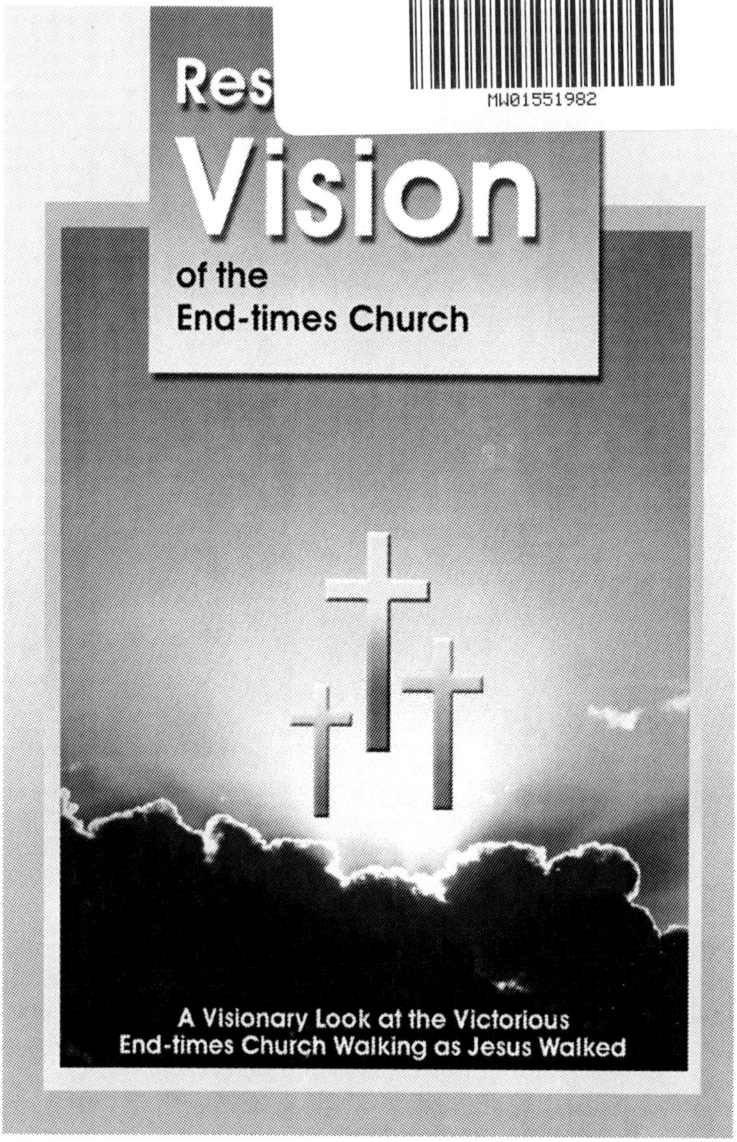

A Visionary Look at the Victorious End-times Church Walking as Jesus Walked

"Making ready a people for the Lord."
Luke 1:17

**2121 Barnes Avenue SE
Salem, OR 97306 USA**

Copyright © 2000
by
Vern Kuenzi

First Printing, January 2001

Published by

**2121 Barnes Avenue SE
Salem, OR 97306 USA**

All rights reserved. No part of this book may be reproduced, translated, stored in a retrieval system or transmitted in any form by any means, whether electronic, mechanical, photocopying, recording or otherwise, without prior written permission from the copyright holder.

Scriptures quoted are from the New American Standard Bible unless otherwise noted. Copyright 1960, 1962, 1963, 1968, 1971, 1972, 1973, 1977, 1987, 1988, The Lockman Foundation.

ISBN 1-929451-01-6
Library of Congress Catalog Card Number 00-133649

Printed in the United States of America

Brackets and bold text and some capitalization in Scripture references are author's insertions for clarity and emphasis.

Dedication

This book is gratefully dedicated in part to my Jewish brethren, many of whom have already paid the ultimate price so that I could be grafted in.

To the trusting saints who have been fed with a humanistic doctrine of the end-times which does not represent what Jesus taught . . . may you be blessed in your search for the truth.

Acknowledgments

Thank You, Lord Jesus, for rescuing me from the pit and giving me this message as a life ministry. Only one thing I ask — that it would glorify You. If in any way it does not, please bring that part to nothing and have mercy on me, a sinner saved only by Your grace.

Celia — dear wife and friend — thank you for your support from start to finish. Thanks for standing without wavering even when I did waver. Sometimes it takes me years to see what you see in minutes. You are a lady without guile.

Nate, if you hadn't shown up at my house and read the manuscript and hadn't volunteered that you would like to publish it, this never would have happened. I had already given up because two big-name publishers had completely ignored the manuscript. So I left it in the hands of the Lord. I believe He hand picked Nate to bring this to completion. You and Joanne and your publishing team have been a blessed providence. I like it when God takes over. His choices are always the right ones.

Half-way around the world God picked Colin, Sandra, Joy, David, and Becky to support this work financially to the exact dollar and the day (which they knew nothing of), and even more importantly, to provide timely encouragement, prayer, and counsel. Bless you, Folks. You are a special gift from God.

I must acknowledge the many saints, both living and dead, who have shared their lives with me and discipled me through their books, tapes, and teachings. In particular, I want to acknowledge Paris Reidhead's short book *Ten Shekels and a Shirt*. The Lord would not let me finish Chapter 2 until I had reread this little book several more times. He obviously wanted to stress the priority of the Glory of God above and beyond all humanistic considerations. It is readily available on the internet.

I would like to acknowledge Reuben Doron's book *One New Man*, ISBN 0-9629049-9-6, published in 1993 by Embrace, Cedar Rapids, Iowa. Some of Chapter 12 is heavily influenced by this book.

I must acknowledge Arthur Katz of Ben Israel Fellowship, LaPorte, Minnesota. The Lord used Art's books and tapes and personal teachings to build a foundation in my early Christian walk that passionately embraced Israel. I owe a heavy debt to his understandings and teachings concerning the holocaust — perhaps a subject that reveals the nature of our God like no other.

Then there are the inspired writings of Watchman Nee. If you haven't yet read *The Normal Christian Life*, please consider it highly recommended. I would like also to acknowledge Sheila Cassidy's book *Sharing the Darkness*, ISBN 971-504-316-X, 1991 Orbis Books, Maryknoll, NY. I was able to find it in the Philippines, and I was reading it when Aunt Lilia died. Sheila planted in my heart the concept of universal redemptive suffering. I know it was of the Lord.

There are literally hundreds of others that I could name. A few that come to mind are John Arnott, Mike Bickle, Paul Billheimer, Paul Cain, Merlin Carrothers, Guy Chevreau, Jack Deere, David Dolan, Francis Fenelon, Charles Finney, Francis Frangipane, Arnold Fruchtenbaum, Madame Guyon, Grant Jeffrey, Rick Joyner, Gary Kah, Robert Van Kampen, Reggie Kelly, R.T. Kendall, Nate Krupp, Hal Lindsey, Martyn Lloyd-Jones, Peter Lord, Andrew Murray, Marvin Rosenthal, Basilea Schlink, Kjell Sjoberg, Hannah Whitall Smith, A.W. Tozer, John White, Smith Wigglesworth, David Wilkerson, and John Wimber. There are others I will wish that I had remembered. In the end, all things will be known. May God bless you, one and all, for your service to the saints. Their listing here, of course, does not imply that they would agree with this writing.

About the Author

Vern Kuenzi was born into a Swiss-German, farming-community family in Silverton, Oregon, on April 21, 1946. When he was six, the family moved to the tiny coastal town of Woods, which is about twenty-five miles south of Tillamook, a town noted for its cheese. He graduated from Cloverdale Grade School, Nestucca Union High School, and in 1968 from Oregon State University with a degree in mechanical engineering. He moved to Hawaii in 1968 where he worked until March 1996 at Pearl Harbor Naval Shipyard. While on work assignment in the Philippines in 1976, he met his lifemate Cecilia Cantero Alphonso. They have lived in Pearl City, Oahu, Hawaii, since 1976.

In 1991, the Lord used the Gulf War to attract, save, and capture Vern for His work and purposes. Vern believes that this message is his life's work and the reason for which he was created. He believes that one day those in religious structure will put him to death, thinking that they are doing God a service, for what is written herein.

Readers are welcomed to visit Vern's website at www.restoringthevision.com.

Preface

This book is not the result of hours of compilation and summary of what others have written, although some of that is here. It is more a result of hours spent walking in the woods seeking the Lord and seeking to understand the mysteries of the book of Revelation and other prophetic books as He would reveal them. I could not scratch the itch within me by doing otherwise. It is based on what I believe the Holy Spirit has shown me on those walks over the last nine years regarding the destiny and call of the Church at the end of this age. Hence it should be read with your Berean cap on, as should any work of that professed origin. It is your responsibility to sift the true from the false. Jesus' first warning was to not be deceived by the false.

This book will probably be largely unpopular and subject to ridicule and rejection because it does not align with the popular end-times doctrines of the day. A remnant, however, will receive it. It is written for you who are that remnant. I do not recommend that you believe what is written here, however, unless you take it before the Lord and obtain witness from the Holy Spirit that it pertains to you. I do not say that because I am concerned that what is written here is false; I say it because truth can come no other way. It is the Holy Spirit Who will lead us into **all** truth. It is my hope and prayer that this writing will prompt you to seek the Lord in your secret place and settle these issues one-on-one with Him. If this book moves you to do that, it will have served its purpose. It would please me if this book could serve as an encouragement and might help you to stand in strength without falling in the days ahead.

There are several chapters that deal with the timing and sequence of end-times events and the identification of key groups. Please do not be stumbled by differences in viewpoints you may have with some of the details presented here. Please do not throw out the *baby* with the *bath water*. It would be presumptuous of me to think that I have all the truth about these things. I certainly see through a glass in various shades of darkness and I hold some of the more subtle details lightly. I have pushed beyond confidence to the point of *probably* or *possibly* in some of these areas in order to try to present a most probable scenario in keeping with the overall vision.

Some who have reviewed this book say that it teaches salvation by works rather than grace. Nothing could be further from my intent. Not only is our salvation by grace, but I believe our sanctification is also by grace. Our job in the process is to recognize our sin and repent of it. Then God's grace forgives us and cleans us from unrighteousness. We have nothing to offer except ourselves as sinful, living sacrifices.

Perhaps this misunderstanding is due to numerous quotes and comments that say suffering and tribulation make us worthy of the Kingdom. We are made worthy because God's purifying grace allows Jesus, Who is worthy, to live in us.

God bless you one and all. Know that He is pleased with your seeking to understand these things.

Foreword

In the spring of 1999, I received a letter from a gentleman in Hawaii named Vern Kuenzi. He said he had read my book *The Church Triumphant at the End of the Age*, agreed with it, and was encouraged by it. He went on to say that he was working on a similar book and would I read the manuscript? In September we were in the Hawaiian Islands conducting several conferences on home church. During our time on Oahu we stayed with Vern and Celia in their home. I was able to look over the manuscript. Not only did I like what I saw, but we began to discuss the possibility of publishing the book.

This is no typical book on how to improve the Church. This is a very strong word to the Body of Christ on what's ahead for God's people. As a theological/Biblical treatise it is one of the best expositions I have seen on the subject of the Church and the end-times. But it is more than that. It is a major prophetic word to the Church about her future. It is a warning that days of persecution and suffering are ahead. But that persecution and suffering is set in the context of God's glory and eternal purpose — and a Church with great purity, authority, power, and anointing.

In Vern's own words, "The Bible says that God's eternal purpose in Christ Jesus and the reason for which He created all things is to demonstrate His wisdom through the Church to the rulers and authorities in the heavenly places . . . the end of this age is not about our fleshly preferences, but His glory. The sooner we embrace His purposes, the sooner we can be about the Father's business of crushing Satan underfoot while being conformed to the likeness of Jesus."

This book is not some short one-night novel. It is weighty. It will take you a while to prayerfully make your way through it. But you will be glad you did. I have never seen a book that is more in God's timing. We at Preparing the Way Publishers consider it a privilege to publish this book. We pray that God will use it around the world to enlighten and prepare His people for the difficult and glorious days ahead. We believe that He will.

Nate Krupp, Publisher
Preparing the Way Publishers

Contents

INTRODUCTION 13

Part One: Restoring the Vision 15

ONE
Is Another Book Necessary? 17

TWO
A Glorious Call; A Grand Plan! 33

THREE
Daniel's Visions of the Cross 41

FOUR
Identifying the Church in Revelation 53

FIVE
Matthew 24 . . . to the Present-day Church? 61

SIX
A Theology of Suffering 73

SEVEN
Restoring the Stolen Vision 97

EIGHT
Follow Me! 111

Part Two: Timing and Sequence of Key Events 127

NINE
The Timing and Sequence of Key Events 129

TEN
Logic Trains of Rapture Timing 151

Part Three: Identification of Key Groups 175

ELEVEN
Who are the Two Witnesses? 177

TWELVE
Who are the Woman and Her Children? 189

THIRTEEN
   Who are the 144,000(s)?...213
FOURTEEN
   Who is the Bride?..223
FIFTEEN
   Holiness and Victory...237

Introduction

Paul reveals the mystery in Ephesians 3:8-12 that God intends to demonstrate His wisdom through the Church to the rulers and authorities in the heavenly places, and that this is the reason for which He created all things and is His eternal purpose in Christ Jesus. The reason Jesus came to earth was to set this plan in motion. 1 John 3:8 says the reason Jesus came was to defeat the works of the devil. He came as a man, lived and died as a man, and became the perfect sacrifice that God needed to legally wrest back from Satan that authority that Adam had turned over. With legal authority over Satan back in the hands of man in the form of the God-Man, Jesus then delegated that authority to His Church to walk out the defeat of Satan by faith.

Restoring the Vision of the End-times Church is an uncompromising call to victory for a Church at the end of this age destined to demonstrate that wisdom of God in the form of the cross of Jesus Christ to the rulers and authorities in the heavenly places. It is a call to endurance rather than an early rapture. It is not a message of *gloom and doom*, but one of joy and victory. It is a call to understand that the Church is destined to overcome Satan by the Blood of the Lamb, the word of her testimony, and by loving not her life unto death. It is a call to the pathway of the cross and, in part, to martyrdom.

There are tremendous parallels between the three and one-half year public ministry of Jesus and the prophetic destiny of the Church during the last three and one-half years of this age. God is going to demonstrate through the corporate body of His Son that wisdom of the cross which He demonstrated 2000 years ago through His Son as an individual. Satan has stolen this glorious call and vision from the Church, and this book seeks to restore that vision and rally the saints to embrace the purposes of God. The Church will be victorious, but the path to victory will be the pathway of the cross.

The term *church* used in this book and as used in the Bible always refers to the remnant blood-bought born-again believers in Jesus Christ who have been transformed by spiritual rebirth into new creatures. It is not referring in the broad ecumenical sense to the religious structure itself or to those who confess Christianity by word of mouth but fail to evidence the reality of the new birth. Consequently, this book will not be received by the majority in the religious structure, but only by those in whom the Holy Spirit dwells and has already been building a foundation of life along the pathway of the cross. These saints will often find the words written here ringing in resonance deep within them, because the Holy Spirit is saying many of the same things to all of us alive at the end of this age. We were born for such a time as this. God bless you, dear brothers and sisters. May you lead many to righteousness in the days ahead and shine like stars forever.

PART ONE

Restoring the Vision

ONE

Is Another Book Necessary?

I believe another book is necessary — one that calls the Church to endurance rather than early rapture. There is little current material in Christian bookstores calling for endurance to the end of the age, but Jesus said to His disciples that those who endure to the end will be saved. That implies that those who do not endure will not be saved. The very end of the age is upon us, and those of us in the Church who are confused over this issue may be in danger of stumbling and even falling away rather than enduring. This grieves me, and I offer this book to the saints with the hope and prayer that hearts may be encouraged and faith may be strengthened, so that we may each finish the race that Jesus has called us to run.

At that Time Many will Fall Away

> For nation will rise against nation, and kingdom against kingdom, and in various places there will be famines and earthquakes. But all these things are merely the beginning of birth pangs. Then they will deliver you to tribulation, and will kill you, and you will be hated by

> all nations on account of My name. And at that time many will fall away and will deliver up one another and hate one another. And many false prophets will arise, and will mislead many. And because lawlessness is increased, most people's love will grow cold. But the one who endures to the end, he shall be saved (Matthew 24:7-13).

Jesus is warning His disciples of a sequence of events at the very end of the age which He compares to birth pains of increasing intensity, during which they will be persecuted and put to death and hated by all nations. These are His words about what lies ahead for His disciples. Those of us who are His disciples and who are alive at the end of this age should expect to see these things. His word settles it. Even though He warned us, many will fall away and the love of most will grow cold. Even though it sounds like a time of desperate hopelessness, it will not be, because a birth is not an event of hopelessness but of expectation and joy. The process, however, is not painless.

> Whenever a woman is in travail she has sorrow, because her hour has come; but when she gives birth to the child, she remembers the anguish no more, for joy that a child has been born into the world (John 16:21).

Jesus did not give these warnings to frighten and discourage us, but rather to warn and encourage us so that we do not stumble and fall away when these inevitable events do come. He has set before us the joy of being birthed as the children of God, but we must endure the birthing process. It was for the joy that lay ahead that Jesus endured the cross. This must also be our attitude as we enter the very end of this age.

> Behold, I have told you in advance (Matthew 24:25).

> These things I have spoken to you, that you may be kept from stumbling (John 16:1).

I offer this book to prepare and encourage my brothers and sisters to endure a time of birthing that, if not anticipated and understood, could result in stumbling and even falling away. I want to share what I believe the Holy Spirit is revealing about these times and their purpose in God's plan for His Church. A birthing as the children of God is in view, and it is a birthing that will result in eternal joy for the saints who endure the temporary — but necessary — birth pains.

Not Gloom and Doom but Joy!

This message is a wake-up call to the Church, but it is not an alarm of *gloom and doom*. It is a message of restoring vision that has been stolen by the enemy. It is a message of God's love. God so loves each of us that He desires to birth us into a bride without spot or wrinkle before Jesus returns. Even though our physical births were not events of *gloom and doom*, they were restrictive, violent, and even bloody events that we as ignorant babes would probably not have chosen had we the choice. The womb was a warm and comfortable place and we would have chosen to remain there in relative comfort and leave well enough alone.

The Church finds herself in this condition as the very end of the age draws near. We are beginning to see and experience the increasing pressures of the birthing process, but we are confused and are seeking a way to avoid it. Paul wrote that the whole creation is groaning, as in the pains of childbirth, for the revealing of the sons of God. He described his own agonizing, as in pains of childbirth, until Christ would be formed in the Galatians. It is the birth of the saints into the likeness of Jesus that is in view in these Scriptures, and we must allow provision at the end of the age for our promised births as the children of God, even though it means enduring the temporary discomfort of birth pains.

A Scriptural Prophetic Teaching

This book is a scriptural prophetic teaching of the glorious call and destiny of the Church at the end of this age. The intent is to identify misleading doctrine and eliminate confusion which might cause saints to stumble and even fall away when these birth pains come. It is also to present what Scripture indicates are the reasons for the majority of the

Church to be on earth at the very end of the age in order to fulfill a glorious calling. It is a common-sense teaching centered on the cross and based on the plain and simple truth of Scripture. I believe that a good portion of it has been illuminated by the Holy Spirit. I consider myself more the delivering postman than the author of this teaching. I am the author, however, of anything that is not of the Holy Spirit. My unsophisticated role in end-times theology could be compared to the role of the child in the crowd in Aesop's fable who cried out, "But the king has no clothes on!" The plain and simple teachings of Jesus about the end of the age have suffered immeasurably by teachings of men that are not in line with what He taught.

If it's not Biblical, it's not Here

Nothing will be presented here that is unscriptural or adds to or subtracts anything from existing Scripture. The issues brought forth will only underscore and illuminate what has already been written. The points that will be presented are prophetic only in that they seek to illuminate existing Scripture based on what I sense the Holy Spirit is freshly revealing. Everything that the Church needs to know about the end of the age in order to endure and emerge victorious has already been given in the Scriptures. We need to study and understand and believe it.

Fresh Insight into Existing Scriptures

Daniel was told that at the end of the age there would be increased understanding of his prophetic visions and dreams. We should expect increased prophetic clarity as the age draws to a close, but we should also anticipate increased prophetic deception as the enemy seeks to stumble the Church on her path to victory. Jesus' first warning to His disciples concerning the end of the age was to beware of deception.

Although the Holy Spirit is giving fresh insight regarding the walk of the Church at the end of the age, this insight is typically at odds with most current end-times Christian literature. Of the multitude of current books dealing with end-times events, only a few place the Church on earth during the final years of the age. Even fewer provide insight into the reasons she is being left on earth and the crucial role she will play in God's eternal plan to restore His creation.

The Church cannot understand and fulfill a major prophetic role on earth at the end of the age if she has no vision to be here. We will study Scriptures which clearly place the Church on earth during the final three and one-half years of the age. We will also study Scriptures which reveal the reasons why she must remain on earth in order to fulfill her glorious prophetic destiny. Rapture timing will become clear as a result of studying these Scriptures and gaining understanding of the destiny to which the Church is called. Rapture timing will be found to be a function of the Church's role on earth and not a cause of it. We will see that the timing of the rapture is not a servant of our personal interests, but of God's eternal glory.

Beware of False Prophetic Voices

We are cautioned that there will be many deceiving voices and false prophets speaking forth at the end of the age. Where there are true prophetic voices, there will always be false ones, even as amidst wheat there will always be tares. We must be as the Bereans, who were commended by Paul as more noble because they judged his words by the Scriptures. This must be more than an intellectual textbook search for facts, as the letter kills but the Spirit gives life. We must rely upon the Holy Spirit to guide us into all truth or we shall surely be deceived. If you do not find this word verified by Scripture and quickened to you personally by the Holy Spirit, you have no reason to believe it.

The voice that spoke through Peter and suggested to Jesus that He need not go to His cross is the same voice speaking through men today and advising the Church that she need not endure to the end of this age and go to her cross. We seem to think that we have already arrived concerning God's ultimate purpose for His Church on earth. But many of the same reasons Jesus chose to endure His cross in order to overcome Satan apply equally to His Church. Satan does not want the Church to fulfill her destiny on earth at the end of this age any more than He wanted Jesus to fulfill His destiny, because his ultimate defeat depends upon both destinies being fulfilled.

It is not conclusive to compile a list of what Bible scholars think about this matter, for most hold different opinions. Truth is not established by vote. Truth about any matter is what God says about it. Personal agendas and doctrines must be set aside, and the Holy Spirit must be solely relied upon to lead us into the truth of what Scripture says about the role of the Church at the end of the age.

We will find that what men teach and what Scripture teaches are often different. But we must decide now that this will not add arms to a battle between believers of different end-times doctrinal beliefs. Our battle is to be against the evil rulers and authorities in heavenly places. Our attack must be on the deception and not on the saints. Doctrine and understanding of the end-times will not move us into or out of the Kingdom of God, but our teachings must not lead the saints along a path which could cause them to stumble and possibly fall away.

A Deceptive Trap

I believe that the Church is being set up for such a stumbling and falling away by teachings which insist that these Scriptures of warning do not apply. These teachings insist that the true Church will have been removed from the earth before these events take place. That is contrary to the plain wording of Scripture. Such teachings unwittingly set a trap in which many saints will be confused and shaken when they find themselves in the midst of events they neither expected nor prepared for. They will be in danger of falling away rather than enduring to the end to which Jesus said we must endure. Jesus would not have warned His disciples to endure to the end of the age in order to be saved if that were not the primary call of the saints alive at the end of the age. Scripture must not be altered to fit our preferred doctrines. Our doctrines must conform to Scripture and, if necessary, be revised until they do.

These seeds of deception have already produced bad fruit. Confusion and difference of opinion, and even apathy among believers, as to the destiny of the Church is common. Some believe they will be momentarily raptured out while others believe they will stay on earth to be victorious and do mighty things. Others believe the point is not important because whatever will happen, will happen. But Paul said, regarding the timing of such events, **"Do not be deceived in any way."** He taught that the issue of timing was of crucial importance, and he went on to carefully describe the timing and nature of end-time events to the church at Thessalonica so that they would not stumble when difficult times came. Paul noted in 2 Timothy 2:18 that false teachings regarding the timing of the resurrection **had already** upset the faith of some. This is proof that proper understanding of the timing of events is important.

Scripture suggests it will be so at the end of this age. False teachings about the timing of the resurrection will result in the upsetting of the faith of many, and many will fall away, spiritually unprepared to endure what must be endured.

Many of us are firmly entrenched in the belief of a rapture which will exclude all of us from the times of turmoil and testing at the end of the age. The teaching of Jesus that **"Those who endure to the end will be saved"** should prompt serious questioning and re-evaluation of that belief. We must search our hearts for hidden motives that overrule the simple truth of His words. The end that Jesus is referring to is the end of this age. Jesus also taught that the harvest would take place at the end of the age. That harvest, as described near the end of Revelation Chapter 14, takes place **after** a specific time of three and one-half years of great tribulation during which believers in Jesus are encouraged to maintain their faith and perseverance. The harvest at the end of this age takes place **after** the great tribulation, not before. We must understand that the Bible clearly teaches that it is **after** the great tribulation of those days that Jesus sends His angels to gather His elect.

Many saints have no vision of being on earth at the end of this age and are banking on an early rapture before the events take place which are described in the prophetic Scriptures of Daniel, Matthew, and Revelation. They are being deceived, however, if they believe that Jesus' warnings to His disciples do not apply to His disciples alive at the end of the age. Any teaching which removes the Church from these Scriptures removes the Church from earth during the most crucial period of her prophetic, earthly destiny.

Satan has Stolen and Twisted the Vision

Scripture says that without vision, people perish (Proverbs 29:18 KJV). If the Church is without vision of her calling at the end of the age, how can she survive to fulfill that calling? If she has been stripped of the vision of the need to endure to the end of the age, how can she endure? In the same voice as Peter we cry, "No way, Lord!" when confronted with the idea of having to endure through tribulation birth pains at the end of the age.

Are we willing to consider a restoration of vision that may violate our doctrinal beliefs and fleshly preferences? You can be assured that Satan has tried to steal and twist that vision, for the outcome of the vision is to see him defeated and crushed underfoot (Romans 16:20). He apparently understands the vision better than we do. He is fighting for his survival, and his only hope is to keep the Church deceived and unaware of her calling, because once the Church grasps her calling and rises to embrace it, he is finished.

We Christians have chosen to turn away from the centrality of the cross and the things of God and have turned to the things of men. We have refused to appropriate the vision of God for His Church at the end of the age, which is that **He has created all things in order to demonstrate His wisdom through the Church to the rulers and authorities in the heavenly places, and that this is His eternal purpose in Christ Jesus** (see Ephesians 3:9-11).

Much current end-times doctrine teaches that the next event on the prophetic calendar is the rapture of the Church. This doctrine teaches that we need only hang on until this event, which could be any day now. I believe this is a deception from the pit of hell designed to prevent the Church from fulfilling her glorious prophetic destiny on earth at the end of the age — a destiny which is to overcome Satan while being conformed to the likeness of Jesus. We are destined to be overcomers, but Satan would have us think otherwise. God has created all things in order to demonstrate His wisdom through His Church to the rulers and authorities in the heavenly places, and those rulers and authorities will do everything in their power and authority to see that the Church does not fulfill this glorious call.

The Nature of the Deception

A. W. Tozer said somewhere in his writings that the more crucial an issue concerning the Church, the more likely the enemy will inject deception and lies into that issue. A perfect example of this is the confusion and controversy surrounding the issue of the destiny of the Church at the end of the age, particularly the rapture issue. We only need to look at the rapture controversy to see the fingerprints of Satan all over it.

Suppose you are presented with two opposing doctrines such as the pre-tribulation rapture scenario and a conflicting one which maintains that the rapture will take place at the harvest at the end of the age. This is a crucial issue, and according to A. W. Tozer's logic, we can conclude that one of these scenarios is either wrong or at least more incorrect than the other. That's just common sense. If one of them is wrong, then we can safely say that Satan is behind it, for Satan is the deceiver, and any important doctrine which concerns the Church and his defeat will be attacked and perverted.

Which scenario is the most probable deception — the one which says the Church will be here during the great tribulation but she is not, or the one which says the Church will not be here but she is? Which one is a trap? Which one has the fingerprints of the deceiver all over it? I would much rather find myself raptured out earlier than expected than to find myself entering a time of great tribulation I neither expected nor prepared for. Wouldn't you?

I don't see a problem with being *over prepared*, but for the sake of discussion, let's assume that all this concern about going through the tribulation is unnecessary and we find ourselves suddenly raptured. I will be elated, even at the expense of having to revise my doctrinal beliefs. I will not stumble and fall away. But what if the rapture doesn't take place until near the end of the last three and one-half years of the age, and we are not prepared to persevere and endure because we have been taught otherwise? The seriousness of doctrinal error is much greater in the latter case. I believe this automatically suggests the place where Satan has set his trap.

We Can't Call the Good News the Bad News

What a tragedy it will be to interpret the events of these times as the wrath of God, when in fact they will be evidence that we are in the process of being birthed and revealed as His sons and daughters. We must not take the good news of Scripture and call it the bad news. We must divide Scripture rightly and embrace the Church's glorious calling and destiny at the end of this age. Our spiritual survival depends on our understanding of these things. We will be in danger of perishing from lack of knowledge and vision if we find ourselves caught up in events at the end of the age for which we have no knowledge and vision. We must understand and be prepared!

BE NOT DECEIVED!

This is a warning cry to the Church to "**BE NOT DECEIVED**" in the days ahead due to a lack of knowledge and vision. We must not be shaken when the world around us begins to teeter and crumble. We must not be shaken when famine, pestilence, warfare, and persecution move in ever closer. We must not think, "Why am I not raptured?" when these events begin to touch our comfortable and sheltered lives. We instead need to welcome them as the beginnings of birth pains which will result in our births into transfigured glory.

This message especially needs to be heard by a complacent and unsuspecting Western Church, because we will be in the greatest danger of falling away when these times of birth pains come to violate our doctrines and upset our sheltered lives.

There Seems to be Provision to Escape . . . through Maturity

There seems to be provision spoken of in Scripture to escape the time of testing that is coming. However, Scripture suggests that relatively few will be found ready and worthy for that escape. There is a group which shows up in heaven at the beginning of Revelation 14 who are identified as first fruits of the harvest. These seem to be those who have matured early. They are described as blameless with no lie in their mouths. But how many stalks of wheat can be held in a hand and waved before the Lord relative to the number of grains of the entire harvest? This is only a first-fruits company, not the majority of the saints. The majority of the saints are called to endure until the harvest at the end of Revelation 14, and that harvest comes after a period of three and one-half years in which the saints are counseled to persevere and not lose their faith in Jesus. It doesn't matter whether these turn out to be saints who have come to faith during the tribulation, or saints who have missed a prior rapture, or saints who are awaiting a rapture that still hasn't come; they are called to persevere and endure to the end.

A Great Multitude of Saints Identified in Great Tribulation!

Those disciples alive as the age ends will very likely be us and/or our children. Scripture clearly identifies a great multitude of saints "that no one could count" in the midst of great tribulation at the end of the age. We obviously won't all escape via a pre-tribulation rapture even if there is one. Perhaps these are those who have missed a prior rapture, but regardless, they are the majority of the Church alive at the end of the age, for it is a **great multitude which no one could count** who emerge victorious from the great tribulation in Revelation 7:9. Scripture does not identify those who will be raptured as a great multitude which no one could count, but rather as "those of us who are alive and remain" (1 Thessalonians 4:15), as if these may be a minority rather than a majority.

Teachings which reassure the Church-at-large of an escape from tribulation through rapture are not accurately representing the plain and simple truth of Jesus' teachings and warnings. Scripture indicates that the majority of the Church, made up of the harvest described at the end of Revelation 14 along with the great multitude of Revelation 7, is going to experience great tribulation to the extent needed to purify and make her worthy of the Kingdom of God. This great multitude of saints from every nation and all tribes and peoples and tongues who come out of the great tribulation, having washed their robes and made them white in the Blood of the Lamb, must have been in the great tribulation in order to be coming out of it. Washed robes made white in the Blood of the Lamb imply a process of purification. Would any of us want to skip that process if it is required to make us worthy of the Kingdom of God?

Scripture clearly gives the reasons why God is allowing a large portion of the Church to remain on earth up to the end of the age. The reasons are to overcome Satan while being purified and made like Jesus. When we understand the glory to which the Church is called, a Church-majority pre-tribulation rapture will seem terribly inconsistent with that call.

The Path that Jesus Walked

Jesus said that in this world we would have tribulation, but not to fear because He has overcome the world. We who are His Church are destined to be victorious over Satan by the Blood of the Lamb, the word of our testimony, and by loving not our lives unto death (Revelation 12:11). God will crush Satan beneath our feet (Romans 16:20). The Church will be victorious! But the path to victory will be along the path that Jesus walked. As He was treated, so we should expect to be treated. Jesus has given us His power and authority to gain this victory, but we can appropriate it only by walking in faith. There is not one way for Him and another way for us, although Satan would have us believe there is. Jesus said, "Follow Me!" Satan will always try to lure us onto other paths.

The Flesh will Resist the Path that Jesus Walked

The flesh is constantly at war with the spirit. Few relish the thought of suffering, even for a worthy cause. It is natural for us to seek a path of comfort and escape from trials, but God knows what is best for His people because He is the Designer of the transformation process. His pattern with His children has always been to transform them by directing their steps along the path that Jesus walked. We are called to embrace the cross, not flee from it. The most formative times in our lives are during times of trial. This is painful for the flesh to hear, but it is God's way. God has chosen to bring restoration to His creation through a process likened to birthing. As a consequence of the fall, birthing involves birth pains. Though the process may be painful, we must look through the pain to the joy beyond. It was for the joy beyond the pain that Jesus endured the cross. The promises of eternal life and reward to the seven churches in the book of Revelation are for the overcomers, not for the cowardly and unbelieving.

God's Love Letter to His Church

The book of Revelation has been described as God's love letter to His Church, because it outlines God's loving plan to conform us to the likeness of His Son. We might question the events described as demonstrating God's love, but we must remember that our Father is bringing forth His transformed children out of a fallen creation. Satan will be overcome and crushed underfoot in the process. The glory of a new creation lies ahead. The process is a birthing, accompanied by necessary birth pains, which reflects the outworking of God's love for His children and their redemption from a fallen state.

An Invitation to Reconsider

I challenge and invite you to take another look at the Scriptures which deal with the plan of God for His Church at the end of the age. I invite you to take yet another look at the Scriptures which deal with the timing of the rapture. It's one thing if the Church won't be here during the birthing process at the end of the age, but it's quite another thing if the Church will be here and these birth pains are hers. We need to seek to understand as much as God has given us in His Scriptures regarding the destiny of His Church.

If God's perfect plan is to take us through such a birthing process, we don't want to be as ignorant babes in the womb who cry out, "No way, Lord!" We need to consent to God's plan for His Church at the end of this age, whatever it is.

Remember, this is not going to be a message of *gloom and doom*, but one of joy and glory. We may not see it that way, because our thoughts about restoration are not always God's thoughts. We must have our minds renewed to align with the eternal purposes of God so that we can endure temporal birth pains for the eternal joy set before us. There is Someone Who has walked this way before Who said, "Follow Me!" It is His own death and resurrection that Jesus compared in John 16:21 to the joyous birth of a child.

It is my prayer that through study of these Scriptures, the Holy Spirit will lead you into a deeper understanding of the call of the Church at the end of the age. It is my prayer that this book will help and encourage those who might otherwise believe that the *true Church* will not be on the earth at the end of the age. It is my prayer that many will be strengthened and encouraged to stand when the inevitable prophesied shakings and testings come. It is my prayer that the faith of many will be strengthened by perceiving the glory to which the Church is called amidst and through the tribulation birth pains which lie ahead. And it is my prayer that our Father may be glorified by a Church who says "Yes!" to His eternal purpose in Christ Jesus which is to demonstrate His wisdom **through the Church** to the rulers and authorities in the heavenly places.

TWO

A Glorious Call; A Grand Plan!

The Glory of God must be the Church's Priority

There is a higher vision than early rapture for the Church as we approach the end of this age, and that is the plan of God for His Church that will demonstrate His wisdom in the sight of all creation to the rulers and authorities in the heavenly places. That plan demands that the Church rise to the full stature that Jesus provided for by the shedding of His priceless blood. This is not about us but about Him. The motives of our desperately wicked, fleshly hearts are always self-serving. We must be given new spiritual hearts. The humanism which has often seeped into our motives must be thrown out and replaced with a love for the glory of God. The motive of our new hearts will be for the glory of God and that the Lamb may receive His just reward for the price He has paid to redeem us. The Church of Jesus Christ was created to glorify and please her Creator.

"Father, lead us in the ways that will please Your heart."

God Created All Things in Order that . . .

When we seek out the eternal plan of God for His Church, no more revealing and awesome Scriptures can be found than Ephesians 3:8-12. In these amazing verses God reveals that He created all things in order to demonstrate His wisdom **through** the Church to the rulers and authorities in the heavenly places. He will be glorified through and before His creation.

> To me, the very least of all saints, this grace was given, to preach to the Gentiles the unfathomable riches of Christ, and to bring to light what is the administration of the mystery which for ages has been hidden in God, **WHO CREATED ALL THINGS; IN ORDER THAT** the manifold wisdom of God might now be made known **THROUGH THE CHURCH** to the rulers and the authorities in the heavenly places. **THIS WAS IN ACCORDANCE WITH THE ETERNAL PURPOSE WHICH HE CARRIED OUT IN CHRIST JESUS OUR LORD**, in whom we have boldness and confident access through faith in Him (Ephesians 3:8-12).

We believe that God created all things. But have we ever considered that He did so with the specific intent of demonstrating His wisdom through the Church to the rulers and authorities in the heavenly places? That should prostrate us on our faces in awe. How is the Church going to do that? Has the Church already finished the demonstration of God's wisdom or is there yet a glorious future fulfillment?

What is the fullness of the eternal purpose spoken of here to be carried out in Christ Jesus our Lord? It is much more than to redeem fallen man for his own sake. Important as that might seem to us, Ephesians 3:8-12 suggests that the redemption of man serves a much higher purpose which has as its final end the glory of God.

Jesus Appeared for what Purpose?

> The Son of God appeared for **THIS** purpose, that He might destroy the works of the devil (1 John 3:8).

This would seem to be the main aspect of the eternal purpose carried out in Christ Jesus in which the redemption of man serves in a supporting role. We were created to assist in destroying the works of the devil. We must be cautious in placing priorities on God's plans, but the Bible suggests that the Church's primary purpose on earth has to do with destroying the works of the devil. Ultimately that will glorify the Father in that His wisdom will be demonstrated through the Church before all creation.

The question continually arises as to why God has allowed evil to flourish on the earth when He could have easily wiped it out at any time. God is more powerful than Satan. It's no contest. So why this delay? **Jesus legally overcame Satan on the cross as a man in order that man could gain the victory over Satan!** Scripture reveals that the eternal purpose of God, which He carried out in Christ Jesus, is to demonstrate His wisdom **through the Church** to the rulers and authorities in the heavenly places. Man gave authority over the earth away through his sin. Man has gained that authority back through the righteous sacrifice of Jesus. 1 Corinthians 1:18-25 defines the wisdom of God as the cross of Jesus Christ. That demonstration of God's wisdom was first modeled by how His Son lived and died while here on earth. The Bible indicates that the wisdom of God, as the cross of Jesus Christ, demonstrated first through His Son two thousand years ago, will again be demonstrated through the corporate body of His Son at the end of this age.

We must understand that God has elected to use His Church to defeat Satan. He has left evil on the earth for the Church to overcome. God sent Jesus to destroy the works of the devil by redeeming a people who would, in the power and authority of His name, defeat Satan by His blood, by the word of their testimony, and by loving not their lives unto death (Revelation 12:11). That is the wisdom of the cross that God will demonstrate through the Church to the rulers and authorities in the heavenly places. This is the glorious calling the Church must embrace. God will be glorified by His Church on earth through the process of the Church defeating Satan by the wisdom of the cross, and we must understand this as our primary earthly calling and the very reason for which we were created. Making disciples of all nations is part of that calling. However, making disciples of all nations is not for the sake of the nations; it is for the glory of God and for the Lamb Who will receive the full reward for the price He has paid.

It is questionable how much of God's wisdom of the cross the Church has demonstrated to date. There have always been individual saints and groups of saints throughout the age who have risen to this calling, but the Church-at-large cannot fully facilitate the fullness of that demonstration until she becomes corporately more like Jesus. She will become corporately more like Jesus when Jesus lives more corporately through her. Scripture indicates that it is not until the Spirit is poured out in fullness during the last three and one-half years of the age that the Church corporately is lifted up by grace to the level needed to fulfill this ultimate calling.

A Glorious Call; A Grand Plan!

I believe the Holy Spirit is saying that during the last three and one-half years of this age a portion of the Church will walk on earth as Jesus walked. Even as Jesus' time of public ministry in the power and authority of the fullness of the Holy Spirit was three and one-half years, so Scripture indicates that the Church will walk in the fullness of His power and authority for that identical length of time. Many in this last-days Church will be called to lay down their lives even as He laid down His life. This will be their path to victory, for it is the Church's destiny to overcome Satan by the Blood of the Lamb, the word of her testimony, and by loving not her life unto death. This is dramatically demonstrated by the victorious life, death, and resurrection of the Lord's two witnesses of Revelation Chapter 11.

Scripture is clear that a large portion of the Church will be on earth during the last three and one-half years of this age, specifically to engage the enemy of our souls in the great final battle between light and darkness. The great tribulation of the last three and one-half years is the final and deciding battle of the ongoing war between Satan and the saints. If Satan can get the Church confused on this issue, he will have won half of the final battle before it begins. Many who are called to be faithful soldiers in the end-times army of God will be in danger of falling away because they will be confused and shaken when they find themselves in the midst of a war they never expected. Now is the time of our spiritual bootcamp. We must be preparing now. We must acquire vision and understanding of our glorious and victorious calling.

The Church was Created for this Most Crucial of Times

It is during this most crucial of times that the final and deciding battle in the war between good and evil will be waged. It makes no sense to think that the Church will not be around for this final battle, when it is for this final battle that the Church was created. To miss this point is to miss the very reason why God created His Church! But we have missed it and have catered to more comfortable agendas while setting aside the eternal purposes of God. We have established doctrinal positions which ignore the plain and simple truth of the Bible.

Satan will be delighted when many fall away during great tribulation because they are unprepared and faithless, having taken as their spiritual food doctrines which have no place for such a scenario.

What we decide by vote is not doctrinal truth. God will do what He said He would do, and in the process He will be glorified through His Church. The question for each of us is which side will we choose? There are two sides and two eternal destinies. We must choose wisely and be willing to pay the price. The path to victory is the path that Jesus walked by way of the cross.

Overcomers by Being Overcome

Scripture indicates that the Church will be victorious and will crush Satan underfoot.

> And the God of peace will soon crush Satan under your feet (Romans 16:20).

However, Scripture further indicates that the path to victory will be by the Church allowing herself to be physically overcome, even as Jesus allowed Himself to be physically overcome on the cross. We will find that the book of Daniel portrays the saints as being victorious and receiving the Kingdom for eternity, but clearly through the process of being physically overcome. This seeming paradox of overcoming by being overcome is the essence of the mystery of the cross.

God is Going to *Do it Again!*

It seems as if God is going to *do it again!* He has already once demonstrated His wisdom of the cross through His Son. He is going to demonstrate His wisdom of the cross again through the corporate body of His Son. Such is the reason for which the Church, and all other things as well, were created. This is the eternal purpose which He chose to carry out in Christ Jesus our Lord. It is the reason why Jesus came as a man to die on the cross.

Perhaps we can now understand more clearly why Jesus rejoiced when He envisioned Satan falling like lightning from heaven. He had just seen His fledgling Church demonstrate the day of small beginnings in His Father's ultimate plan to crush Satan underfoot. No wonder Jesus rejoiced. His purpose in coming was to defeat the works of Satan, and He was seeing the beginning of the working out of that perfect plan. The Son's heart was thrilled, for He surely sensed the good pleasure of His Father.

> And He said to them, "I was watching Satan fall from heaven like lightning. Behold, I have given you authority to tread upon serpents and scorpions, and over all the

power of the enemy, and nothing shall injure you. Nevertheless do not rejoice in this, that the spirits are subject to you, but rejoice that your names are recorded in heaven." At that very time He rejoiced greatly in the Holy Spirit, and said, "I praise Thee, O Father, Lord of heaven and earth, that Thou didst hide these things from the wise and intelligent and didst reveal them to babes. Yes, Father, for thus it was well-pleasing in Thy sight" (Luke 10:18-21).

The Church's Calling is to Fulfill this Destiny While on Earth

A Church-majority, pre-tribulation rapture does not fit into this scenario. It is a great multitude that no one could count who are identified in Revelation Chapter 7 as emerging victoriously from great tribulation. It is through the Church on earth that God will demonstrate His wisdom to the devil and his angels. Satan has tried and continues to try to distort this truth for his own purposes.

We need to seek God's purposes for our lives and understand the reason for which we, who are alive at the end of this age, were created. Perhaps we were created for such a time as this. We were created to be overcomers, conformed to the likeness of Jesus while crushing Satan underfoot by the wisdom of the cross. Let us seek not only to understand but to embrace the purposes of God for His Church at the end of this age.

Not *When* but *Why?*

Although rapture timing is a hot issue in current end-times Christian literature, our primary concern at the end of this age is not whether the rapture will be pre-tribulation, post-tribulation, mid-tribulation, pan-tribulation, or pre-wrath. Our concern should be how God will maximize His glory through His Church brought to full stature in His Son. If the Church's presence on earth at the end of the age is involved in that glorification, then the Church should expect and desire to be here. God has established His Church and her destiny on earth in accordance with His eternal purpose, which is to demonstrate His wisdom through her to the rulers and authorities in the heavenly places. This is the foundational truth on which our end-times doctrine regarding the Church should rest.

"Father, let this understanding sink deep into our spirits and ignite the revelation of Your individual calling for each of us. Lead us on to victory in the power and authority of Jesus' name to Your everlasting Glory! May we glorify You by our lives and deaths in the outworking of Your eternal plan. Father, have Your way with us, vessels of clay astonishingly designed to glorify You by allowing the demonstration of Your wisdom of the cross through us."

THREE

Daniel's Visions of the Cross

As the Waters of Mystery Recede, the Cross is Revealed

As the waters of mystery recede, the highest peaks of revelatory truth are first to emerge. What the Bible reveals at first is always of foundational importance to all that follows. The dreams and visions given the prophet Daniel are the highest peaks of revelatory truth regarding the destiny of the saints. No additional future revelation ever diminishes their relative height and importance, but only reveals their base to a broader extent. These initial truths reveal the primary destiny and calling of the saints at the end of the age and must be kept as the basis of our understanding of all that follows as the destiny of the saints becomes further clarified in the book of Revelation.

The content of the prophetic dreams and visions of Daniel has been taught by some as applicable only to the literal nation of Israel and not to the Church. It is true that the people described in Daniel's revelations are not referred to as the Church, but as the *saints of the Highest One, your people,* or the *holy people.* Even in the book of Revelation, groups of people are frequently referred to as *saints* and not identified by the term *church*. However, these groups in Revelation can be identified as the Church based on their relationship to Jesus Christ. The book of Daniel does not identify these groups of people based on their relationship to Jesus. Therefore, Daniel's dreams and visions must be interpreted in the light of further insight given in the book of Revelation and other New Testament Scriptures in order to apply them to the Church.

We will see that the *saints* and *your people* and the *holy people* of Daniel's dreams and visions match exactly the saints in the book of Revelation. The period of time in view in both books is the final three and one-half years of the age. The book of Revelation clearly identifies these saints as followers of Jesus Christ. This must be understood in order to apply the critical foundational prophecies of Daniel to the Church and not consider them as applicable only to literal Israel. Daniel understood the *saints* and *your people* and the *holy people* to be the Jewish people. He was right, but his understanding was limited to the Jewish portion of the eventual one-new-man company known as the Church which would consist of both Jewish and Gentile believers.

Daniel's Dreams and Visions

Daniel received a succession of dreams and visions crucial to our understanding of the destiny of the Church. He had difficulty comprehending this because of the measured extent of the revelation given him, and because he could only process it with his Old Testament theology. The revelations he received were so staggering to his understanding that at one point he became ill. He was looking forward in time and seeing the Church of Jesus Christ at the end of the age, specifically during the last three and one-half years of the age. He had no knowledge of a future Church or of a suffering Savior. Yet his dreams and visions are a clear prophetic picture of the destiny of the Church at the end of the age.

Each succeeding dream or vision builds upon previous revelations even as the book of Revelation builds upon the book of Daniel. The information given by all of these prophetic revelations needs to be pieced together in order to build an accurate picture regarding the destiny of the Church. Any piece of the puzzle left out or misapplied will result in an incomplete and inaccurate picture. Daniel was specifically told that he would not understand the things he was shown, but that he was to write them down to be preserved for — and understood by — a people alive at the time of the end.

Daniel's Little Book is Now Open!

One of the strongest impressions that I ever received from the Holy Spirit regarding the study of these prophetic Scriptures concerned the little book in Daniel 12. The Holy Spirit seemed to say that the little book of Daniel 12, ordered sealed up until the time of the end, is the same little book that reappears opened in the hands of the angel in Revelation 10:2. The description of the last three and one-half years of the age, which was the topic of discussion of Daniel 12, is again the topic of discussion following the opening of the little book in Revelation 10. When the visions of Daniel and John are combined, a complete picture of the destiny of the Church at the end of the age emerges.

Daniel's Vision in the First Year of Belshazzar

Daniel Chapter 7 describes a vision involving a succession of four strange beasts which represent empires.

> These great beasts, which are four in number, are four kings who will arise from the earth. But the saints of the Highest One will receive the kingdom and possess the kingdom forever, for all ages to come (Daniel 7:17-18).

The outcome of this vision is that the saints of the Highest One will one day receive the Kingdom and possess it forever, for all ages to come. These verses describing the first vision of Daniel are foundational to all that follows. Nothing is said to Daniel about who these saints are or how this comes to pass. This is the first revelatory peak to emerge as the waters of mystery recede.

Daniel asked for additional insight and was given further revelation regarding the beast empires and the saints.

> I kept looking, and that horn was waging war with the saints and overpowering them until the Ancient of Days came, and judgment was passed in favor of the saints of the Highest One, and the time arrived when the saints took possession of the kingdom (Daniel 7:21-22).

> And he [the little horn] will speak out against the Most High and wear down the saints of the Highest One, and he will intend to make alterations in times and in law; and they will be given into his hand for a time, times and half a time [three and one-half years]. But the court will sit for judgment, and his dominion will be taken away, annihilated and destroyed forever. Then the sovereignty, the dominion, and the greatness of all the kingdoms under the whole heaven will be given to the people of the saints of the Highest One; His kingdom will be an everlasting kingdom, and all the dominions will serve and obey Him (Daniel 7:25-27).

Notice that this additional revelation adds details indicating that the saints will be warred against, that they will be worn down, and that they will be given into the hand of a "little horn" (commonly understood to be the antichrist) for a period of three and one-half years. Nevertheless, they will emerge victorious. This is a crucial additional piece of data regarding the prophetic destiny of the saints at the end of the age. The saints will be victorious, **but** that path to victory will be through a process of being warred against and worn down. This is the second revelatory peak to emerge as the waters of mystery continue to recede.

Daniel's Vision in the Third Year of Belshazzar

Daniel received additional revelation in this vision indicating that the holy people would not only be warred against and worn down, but that they would be destroyed.

> And his [the antichrist's] power will be mighty, but not by his own power, and he will destroy to an extraordinary degree and prosper and perform his will; **he will destroy mighty men and the holy people** (Daniel 8:24).

Daniel's Vision in the Third Year of Cyrus

Chapters 10 through 12 reveal Daniel's last vision concerning the saints at the end of the age.

> And I heard the man dressed in linen, who was above the waters of the river, as he raised his right hand and his left toward heaven, and swore by Him who lives forever that it would be for a time, times, and half a time [three and one-half years]; and as soon as they finish **shattering the power of the holy people,** all these events will be completed. As for me, I heard but could not understand; so I said, "My lord, what will be the outcome of these events?" And he said, "Go your way, Daniel, for these words are concealed and sealed up until the end time. Many will be purged, purified and refined; but the wicked will act wickedly, and none of the wicked will understand, but those who have insight will understand" (Daniel 12:7-10).

The age will end in a specific period of three and one-half years during which the power of the holy people will be shattered. These *holy people* are the same people previously referred to as the *saints*. They are warred against, worn down, shattered, and destroyed — yet emerge victorious as recipients of the Kingdom. It is the process of being purged, purified, and refined that has transformed these saints, who have been warred against, into the holy people. That is the essence of the destiny of the saints portrayed in the book of Daniel.

The New Testament, and most specifically the book of Revelation, builds upon these foundational revelations and applies them clearly to the Church on earth at the end of the age. But nowhere else is the path of victory for the Church so clearly described as in the book of Daniel where it is described as a process of being physically destroyed. The first two peaks are further revealed as the waters of mystery continue to recede, and the contents of the little book, reopened in the book of Revelation, are exposed.

The Saints of Daniel are the Saints of Revelation

The third revelatory peak to emerge, as Daniel's little book is opened in Revelation Chapter 10, is that the saints of Daniel and the saints of Revelation are one and the same. They are destined to be **physically destroyed** for the express purpose of overcoming Satan thereby demonstrating God's wisdom through the Church to the rulers and authorities in the heavenly places.

> And there was given to him a mouth speaking arrogant words and blasphemies; and authority to act for forty-two months [three and one-half years] was given to him. And he opened his mouth in blasphemies against God, to blaspheme His name and His tabernacle, that is, those who dwell in heaven. And it was given to him [the antichrist] to make war with the saints and to overcome them; and authority over every tribe and people and tongue and nation was given to him. And all who dwell on the earth will worship him, everyone whose name has not been written from the foundation of the world in the book of life of the Lamb who has been slain. If anyone has an ear, let him hear. If anyone is destined for captivity, to captivity he goes; if anyone kills with the sword, with the sword he must be killed. Here is the perseverance and the faith of the saints (Revelation 13:5-10).

The Saints of Daniel and Revelation are the Church

The fourth peak to emerge from the waters of mystery is that the saints of Daniel are not only the saints of Revelation, but that they are the Church of Jesus Christ. The identity of the saints of Daniel is forever settled by their relationship with Jesus as revealed in the following verses:

> And another angel, a third one, followed them, saying with a loud voice, "If anyone worships the beast and his image, and receives a mark on his forehead or upon his hand, he also will drink of the wine of the wrath of God, which is mixed in full strength in the cup of His anger; and he will be tormented with fire and brimstone in the presence of the holy angels and in the presence of the Lamb . . . Here is the perseverance of the **saints** who keep the commandments of God **and their faith in Jesus.**" And I heard a voice from heaven, saying, "Write, 'Blessed are the dead who die **in the Lord** from now on!'" "Yes," says the Spirit, "that they may rest from their labors, for their deeds follow with them" (Revelation 14:9-10,12-13).

The Mystery and Paradox of the Cross

The mystery of the cross was revealed to Daniel, although he did not understand what he had seen and heard. He had no historical pattern in which a people could be victorious through a process of being worn down, shattered, and destroyed. And yet he was given a revelation of a holy people at the end of the age who are ultimately victorious through such a process — a process that he could only understand as total defeat. It suggests the appearance of total defeat that Jesus must have displayed as He hung shattered and destroyed on the cross.

This is a glimpse of the Church at the end of the age walking the path that Jesus walked. It may be as confusing and disconcerting to us as it was to Daniel, even though Daniel's little book has been reopened for our reading. However, much of our current theology and teaching avoids the foundational truths of the cross. Some will disassociate those saints who are overcome at the end of the age from those in the seven churches in Revelation who are called to be overcomers. The essence of the cross, however, is that one overcomes by laying down one's life, sometimes physically.

Those saints who **are** physically overcome are the same saints who **do** spiritually overcome.

I Heard but Could not Understand

Daniel was staggered to the point of illness by these revelations. The Church must understand that she will be victorious, but her path to victory at the very end of the age, as mapped out in the book of Daniel, involves her physical destruction. Such a destiny seems bitter to us and impossible to swallow. Do we also hear but fail to understand?

We will never be able to embrace this destiny without the mind of Christ. Only for the joy set before us, in valid eternal perspective, will we be able to accept and endure these things. The cross of Christ is the wisdom of God because God established it as His wisdom; it does not depend on our understanding or lack of it. He said it; that settles it. Pray that we may have our minds renewed to understand this awesome destiny and that God may give us the grace to both embrace it and endure.

Living Out the Sermon on the Mount

This is a living demonstration of the theology of the Sermon on the Mount. It is the life that Jesus lived. It is the wisdom of the cross. Wasn't His path to victory through allowing Himself to be physically overcome? The churches in Revelation are counseled to be overcomers, yet the paths of some of the overcomers in the church of Smyrna clearly led to being physically overcome (martyred). There is no inconsistency with the *overcomers* also being *overcome*. We must, however, differentiate between being *spiritually overcome* and being *physically overcome*. The definition of being *spiritually overcome* would involve falling away and receiving the mark of the beast. We must not be overcome in that manner.

Although it appears a paradox, it is not a paradox in light of the wisdom of God which is the wisdom of the cross. What makes it a paradox in our minds is that we often think with the minds of men, as Peter did, when in honest good intention he counseled Jesus not to go to the cross. The wisdom of man, which is diametrically opposed to the wisdom of God, is that we overcome by striking back and by vindicating ourselves. But the wisdom of God is the cross of Christ, whereby Jesus allowed Himself to be overcome in the flesh to the point of death. He never struck back. He never opened His mouth to vindicate Himself. In this manner, He won the victory. We are called to do the same and to again demonstrate the wisdom of the cross. This is the wisdom that God will demonstrate through the Church. It will overcome evil and re-establish righteous rule over all of creation for eternity.

The *paradox* of the conflict is revealed by balancing two separate verses from the book of Revelation.

> And **they** overcame **him** because of the blood of the Lamb and because of the word of their testimony, and **they** did not love their life even to death (Revelation 12:11).

> And it was given to **him** to make war with the **saints** and to overcome **them**; and authority over every tribe and people and tongue and nation was given to **him** (Revelation 13:7).

The *him* in these verses is Satan or his antichrist. The *they* and the *them* are the saints who are the Church. The saints are both overcome and overcomers through the same event.

Holy and Powerful

There are two additional points which reveal that the saints of Daniel are the Church. Notice from the context of Daniel 12:7 that the saints at the end of the age are **holy** and **powerful**, even though they are warred against and overcome. Who or what must be the source of the holiness and power of these saints? Can there be any source of holiness and power at the end of the age other than Jesus? We know that Satan is powerful, but he is not holy. The combination of holiness and power can only be supplied by Jesus Christ. The only way these saints can be holy and powerful is if Jesus is living in them and exhibiting **His** holiness and power through them. These must be the Church. We should not be surprised, therefore, to find these same saints identified in the book of Revelation as the Church of Jesus Christ.

Recipients of the Kingdom

The second point is that these saints of Daniel are recipients of the Kingdom. With the benefit of the New Testament, we understand that followers of Jesus will receive the Kingdom. Therefore, these saints in view at the end of the age must also be followers of Jesus.

> Do not be afraid, little flock, for your Father has chosen gladly to give you the kingdom (Luke 12:32).

> Listen, my beloved brethren: did not God choose the poor of this world to be rich in faith and heirs of the kingdom which He promised to those who love Him (James 2:5)?

> Therefore, since we receive a kingdom which cannot be shaken, let us show gratitude, by which we may offer to God an acceptable service with reverence and awe; for our God is a consuming fire (Hebrews 12:28-29).

> And turning His gaze on His disciples, He began to say, "Blessed are you who are poor, for yours is the kingdom of God" (Luke 6:20).

The foundational truth revealed in Daniel is that the Church will be victorious and receive the Kingdom through the process of being *warred against* and *worn down* and *overcome*. Nowhere do we read of the option of escape from this process. If there is an option of escape, perhaps it will be revealed further along. For now we have to understand that this call is primary. It is equally as primary for the Church at the end of the age as it was for Jesus — for all but one of the same reasons, as we shall see.

There is a strong natural tendency to identify ourselves with a group that is protected and exempt from the onslaught of Satan during the great tribulation. And in a sense we are exempt, because Jesus prayed that we would be kept safe from the evil one. However, *being kept safe* in that context has nothing to do with preserving our physical lives. God is more concerned with our billions of years in eternity than with our seventy years of earthly life, and so should we be concerned. The safety that Jesus is referring to is in the context of spiritual safety, not physical safety. The **martyrs** in Smyrna are told that they will not be hurt by the *second death*. Their first death is not of eternal consequence, but their potential second one is. Jesus said in Luke 21:16-18 that some of us will be put to death, but not a hair of our heads would perish. The primary call of the saints as described in the book of Daniel is physical destruction. The two foundational truths regarding the walk of the Church at the end of the age are that she will be victorious and receive the Kingdom, but through the process of being physically overcome to the extent of being shattered and destroyed.

Regardless of the validity of exceptions to this primary call, it is a multitude so great that no one could count them that emerges victorious from the great tribulation in Revelation 7. We will see that the logical sequence and context of events identify these as martyred saints, not raptured ones.

When Jesus said "Follow Me," He was not inviting us to the presidential suite of the King David Hotel. He was inviting us to join Him in reproach and death outside the camp. If the nature of our call is significantly different than this, why were the foundational apostles, with the possible exception of John, martyred even as their Lord was? It is said that the Church was birthed through the blood of the martyrs. Apparently the Church will grow to maturity as well through the blood of the martyrs, for we will see that it is the death of the saints at the end of the age that ushers in the time when the bride is at last declared ready.

Demonstration of the Mystery

This scenario is most clearly demonstrated by the life, death, and subsequent resurrection of the two witnesses of Revelation Chapter 11. They are said to be *overcome*, but they are classic examples of those who *do overcome* as a consequence of allowing themselves to be *overcome*. These two witnesses are witnesses of the Lord Jesus Christ and represent the Church at peak power and authority. They are holy and powerful. Yet they are warred against, overcome, and killed. Three and one-half days later they are resurrected to heaven. This is a snapshot of victory after being overcome! This is a demonstration of overcoming after being overcome! Saints, may all of our destinies be so glorious!

FOUR

Identifying the Church in Revelation

We have seen how Daniel received a series of visions, each building upon the previous, and yet he could not understand what it all meant, for he was given only a portion of the overall picture. He was told that the words he had received were to be concealed and sealed up until the end-time. We are now in that end-time and have the benefit of New Testament Scripture, including John's visions in the book of Revelation. The little book that was sealed up in Daniel Chapter 12 until the time of the end is now open in the hands of the angel in Revelation Chapter 10. The events of the last three and one-half years of the age regarding the calling and destiny of the Church are revealed for our understanding.

However, many teach that the Church is not in view in Revelation Chapters 5 through 19 because the word *church* is nowhere to be found. Conclusions are drawn that the Church must have been raptured before the events described in these chapters take place. But is that what the Bible really teaches?

Are the Saints in Revelation Chapters 5 through 19 the Church?

It is not necessary that the actual word *church* be found in Revelation Chapters 5 through 19 to keep from identifying the people groups described as the *Church*. There are descriptions in these chapters of groups who follow the Lamb wherever He goes, who are dressed in white robes standing before the throne, who stand before their Lord, and who follow the commandments of God and believe in Jesus Christ. People are the Church based on their relationship to Jesus Christ, regardless of whether they are called the saints, the elect, the multitudes, or whatever — regardless of rapture timing.

Chapters 5 through 19 of the book of Revelation clearly identify the Church on earth in the midst of the events described and could not be any clearer short of using the actual word *church*. I fear that this is one of those times in which we are seeking support of our established doctrines rather than the simple truth of Scripture. We don't want to see the Church in these chapters because it wouldn't fit in with our beliefs. **The book of Revelation is written to the Church, for the Church, and about the Church; and the content of Chapters 5 through 19 is the very heart of the prophetic destiny of the Church on earth at the end of the age.** We may not like it, but that doesn't change it. We must adapt doctrine to Scripture, not vice versa.

The companion teaching along this line is that the twenty-four elders described in Revelation 4:4 are the Church raptured before the tribulation begins. Notice, however, that these twenty-four elders continue to exist as a separate group of twenty-four individuals, even when the various factions of the Church assemble themselves in heaven up to and including Chapter 19. If these twenty-four elders represent the Church, they certainly do not represent the bulk of the Church. They are twenty-four individuals, not a multitude that no one could count. We must not designate a specific group as the Church where it is not clearly identified, while at the same time ignoring it where it is clearly identified.

Relationship with Jesus Identifies Us as the Church

The Church is plainly described in Revelation Chapters 5 through 19, but not by the word *church*. The following various groups are identified as portions of the Church because of their clear relationship to Jesus Christ:

- Under the altar at the fifth seal in Chapter 6, we see the souls of those who have been slain because of the word of God and because of the testimony they had maintained. This identifies them as a portion of the Church. The word of God is the gospel of Jesus Christ. It is the testimony of Jesus Christ that gets people in trouble, just as Jesus said it would.

- At the sixth seal in Chapter 7, we find a great multitude, so vast that no one could count them, appearing in heaven having come out of the great tribulation. They are identified as having washed their robes and made them white in the **Blood of the Lamb.** These are obviously a portion of the Church.

- The two witnesses of Chapter 11, who prophesy standing before the Lord of the earth and are described as lying dead in the streets of the great city where also **their Lord** was crucified and are then taken up to heaven, are obviously part of the Church.

- The saints of Chapter 14, whom the beast wars against and who are encouraged to keep the commandments of God and their faith **in Jesus,** are obviously part of the Church.

- Those harvested at the end of Chapter 14, who are heard in heaven singing the song of Moses and the **song of the Lamb** having emerged victorious over the beast and his image and the number of his name, are obviously part of the Church.

All of these groups are found in Chapters 5 through 19, and they all fit descriptions of portions of the Church based on their relationship to Jesus Christ. The bride is revealed in Chapter 19 having made herself ready at last. She didn't just jump there from Chapter 5. She has been implicitly involved in the purification and refining processes mentioned in Chapters 5 through 19. The white linen she is clothed in is described as the righteous acts of the saints. She is, at least in part, made up of those saints who have just emerged victorious from the great tribulation.

The Church is found everywhere in the book of Revelation. She achieves bride status as she is purified by the crucible of events during the last three and one-half years of the age. Jesus is coming back for a bride without spot or wrinkle, and one of the purposes of the great tribulation is clearly portrayed as helping to establish that purity. Logically then, our only hope of escape from these times is to be found without spot or wrinkle before these times begin.

To the Churches, for the Churches

> John to the seven churches . . . (Revelation 1:4).

> I, Jesus, have sent My angel to testify to you these things for the churches (Revelation 22:16).

These things are written to the Churches and for the Churches. It is to the Churches that the book of Revelation was written. It is for the Churches that the book of Revelation was written. It is about the Churches that the book of Revelation was written. God will demonstrate His wisdom through the Church to the rulers and authorities in the heavenly places. This description of the destiny and calling of the Church is what Chapters 5 through 19 of the book of Revelation are all about.

God will be glorified by His Church — on earth — through the events at the end of this age, and we must come into agreement with His plan as clearly defined by these Scriptures. The heart of the walk of the Church is contained in these chapters, and to remove the Church from them is to pull the vision for the Church out of Scripture and discard it. It is in Chapters 5 through 19 that we find described the process for the victory of the saints over Satan. It is in Chapters 5 through 19 that we find the witness of the Church in its finest hour and the completion of the great commission to take the gospel to the entire world. Yes, we find great tribulation there. But in that great tribulation we see the purification process that results in the emergence of the bride, having made herself ready. I hope you grasp how crucial this portion of the book of Revelation is to the call and destiny of the Church at the end of the age. I fear that only Satan's best interests are served by removing the Church from what is described in these chapters. I believe it would be good to prayerfully consider our Lord's words of warning given in Revelation 22:18-19 regarding taking away from or adding anything to these Scriptures.

A Deception must be Called a Deception

These are hard words. I am sometimes tempted to edit them out or soften them because I know some will be offended by them. But I believe they are appropriate. My motive is to wake up saints who might otherwise be led unprepared into a situation at the end of this age which could cause them to stumble and fall away. The salvation of a soul is worth more than the risk of offending someone by violating their doctrinal beliefs.

Any terminology that calls a real deception less than a deception is in itself a deception. Paul used the term *deception* regarding false teaching on the timing of the day of the Lord, and Jesus turned to Peter and identified Satan as the voice urging Him not to go to the cross. Satan is the deceiver, and it is Satan who is behind any false teaching regarding the role of the Church at the end of the age. Hence I choose to call any teaching, which does not identify the Church in Revelation Chapters 5 through 19, a deception from the enemy designed to deceive the saints and keep them from fulfilling their glorious destiny at the end of the age — that is to be transformed into the likeness of Jesus and to see Satan crushed underfoot. Any teaching which detracts from what Scripture says regarding this process can only be in the best interests of the enemy of our souls.

However, I want to re-emphasize that this is not intended in any way to be an attack on the saints who teach, and who have taught, the pre-tribulation doctrine. It is an attack on the doctrine itself which does not agree with the common-sense teaching of Scripture. Many great men of God have believed in and taught this pre-tribulation doctrine and continue to teach it. We only see what we have been given to see. Believing in or teaching a pre-tribulation rapture will not bar anyone from entering the eternal city. We will be barred from the eternal city, however, if we fail to endure because we believed a false teaching and fell to the temptation to receive the mark of the beast. Therefore, let us be aware of the potential danger in the pre-tribulation teaching which could impact our very salvation. We are counseled to be wise as serpents while gentle as doves.

The pre-tribulation teaching does have an element of truth in it, because we will see that the Bible teaches that holiness and maturity does keep some of the Church from the hour of testing. However, the commonly taught rapture of all believers before tribulation starts is just not accurate. Furthermore, Scripture teaches that the rapture is not at the beginning of the final seven years of the age. We must understand that God is going to use great tribulation to transform His saints into the likeness of Jesus. Some will not have to be purified in that crucible, but Scripture indicates that most of the Church who are alive at the end of this age will require this purification. It is **a great multitude that no one could count** who emerge victoriously from the great tribulation in Revelation 7:14.

"Father, would You have mercy on all of us who attempt to teach these things, and would You lead us in Your ways, granting us wisdom and revelation to help the saints rather than hinder them. Father, would You bring to nothing all the attempts of the enemy to deceive the Church in these areas, and would You give wisdom and revelation to the

Church to see these matters as You see them? In Jesus' name, we ask this, for Your glory, and for the sake of the saints who will be alive at the end of the age."

FIVE

Matthew 24 . . . to the Present-day Church?

Comfortable but False Reassurances

Christian bookstores are plentifully supplied with reassuring books that Matthew 24 does not apply to the *true Church*, and that a rapture will remove the *true Church* prior to the events described. Those who are not the *true Church*, or those who come to Christ after the rapture, will be left behind to suffer and endure these persecutions.

Jesus taught otherwise. He taught His disciples that as He was hated by the world, so they would be hated, and that as He was persecuted, so they would be persecuted. He told them that an hour was coming when those who killed them would think that they were offering God a service. He told His disciples that He was telling them these things specifically so that they would not stumble when these things happened. He told His disciples that those who endured to the end would be saved. He did not even mention an optional plan.

YOU will Experience these Things

We have just understood from studying Daniel that the primary calling of the Church at the end of the age is to overcome Satan by allowing herself to be physically overcome, even as Jesus allowed Himself to be physically overcome. The birth pains described in Matthew 24 are part of that process. When Peter, James, John, and Andrew questioned Jesus privately about when the temple would be destroyed, what would be the sign of His coming, and what would be the sign of the end of the age, He answered them in terms that uneducated fishermen could understand. He warned them not to be misled by false Christs. He warned them not to be alarmed by wars, famines, and earthquakes, but that these things were the beginning of birth pangs.

He warned that they would be delivered to tribulation, would be killed, and would be hated by all nations on account of His name. He warned about a great falling away, the arising of many false prophets who would lead many astray, and the increase of lawlessness which would cause most people's love to grow cold. And He told them to their faces that *YOU* will experience these things.

> See to it that no one misleads **YOU**. And **YOU** will be hearing of wars and rumors of wars; see that **YOU** are not frightened . . . Then they will deliver **YOU** to tribulation, and will kill **YOU**, and **YOU** will be hated by all nations on account of my name . . . Therefore when **YOU** see the abomination of desolation . . .

They are Jesus' most serious warnings to His disciples about what they should expect at the end of the age. These warnings were not spoken to the multitudes, but privately to His disciples. It would be a serious mistake for any of His disciples to ignore or misapply such warnings. The enemy of our souls would, of course, love to see that happen. And that is exactly what he has attempted with the development and distribution of teachings that say that we will all be raptured before these events of Matthew 24 take place. Jesus did not say that His Church would be raptured before these events take place. As we have seen, He said:

> But the one who endures to the end, he shall be saved (Matthew 24:13).

If there were another path which would preclude the majority of the Church alive at the end of the age from experiencing these things, wouldn't Jesus have told the foundational apostles of His Church? He didn't mention how to escape these things, but how to endure them. These are Jesus' teachings about what His Churches should expect, specifically applicable to the Church at the end of the age. Nevertheless, the Church relies on teachings saying we won't have to endure to the end of the age because a rapture could occur any day now. Jesus goes on to state that the end would come only after the gospel had been preached world-wide, and only after a great tribulation which would eliminate all life on earth unless it was cut short. Only then did He say:

> and then the sign of the Son of Man will appear in the sky, and then all the tribes of the earth will mourn, and they will see the Son of Man coming on the clouds of the sky with power and great glory. And He will send forth His angels with a great trumpet and they will gather together His elect from the four winds, from one end of the sky to the other (Matthew 24:30-31).

Who are the Elect?

Who exactly is Jesus warning, and who are these elect that will be gathered? Are they only Jewish because the first disciples were Jewish, and because mention is made in Verse 16 of those in Judea? Or are these things written and applicable to the entire Church, Jewish and Gentile, in addition to His contemporary Jewish disciples? Could there be a prior rapture that Jesus didn't mention that makes all of this irrelevant to the present-day Church?

The plain sense of the wording of Scripture is that Matthew 24 is written and applicable to all of Jesus' disciples, the elect/chosen Jews and Gentiles throughout the age. Those specific elect living at the end of the age should plan to endure to the harvest at the end of the age in order to be saved.

It is for the sake of these elect mentioned in Matthew 24, Verses 22, 24, and 31, that the great tribulation will be cut short. It is these elect that Satan is trying to deceive because it is these elect who will fully demonstrate God's purpose for the Church on earth at the end of the age. It is these elect left alive who will be gathered by Jesus' angels after the end of the great tribulation.

> And unless those days had been cut short, no life would have been saved; but for the sake of the **elect** those days shall be cut short (Matthew 24:22).

> And He will send forth His angels with a great trumpet and they will gather together His **elect** from the four winds, from one end of the sky to the other (Matthew 24:31).

Chosen and *elect* are of the same Greek root and apply to the entire born-again Church at the end of the age. This is clear when other Scriptures speaking of the chosen and elect are considered.

> And unless the Lord had shortened those days, no life would have been saved; but for the sake of the **elect** whom He chose, He shortened the days (Mark 13:20).

> For this reason I endure all things for the sake of those who are **chosen,** that they also may obtain the salvation which is in Christ Jesus and with it eternal glory (2 Timothy 2:10).

> Peter, an apostle of Jesus Christ, to God's **elect,** strangers in the world, scattered throughout Pontus, Galatia, Cappadocia, Asia and Bithynia, who have been **chosen** according to the foreknowledge of God the Father, through the sanctifying work of the Spirit, for obedience to Jesus Christ and sprinkling by His blood: Grace and peace be yours in abundance (1 Peter 1:1-2 NIV).

> These will wage war against the Lamb, and the Lamb will overcome them, because He is Lord of lords and King of kings, and those who are with Him are the called and **chosen** and faithful (Revelation 17:14).

> What then? That which Israel is seeking for, it has not obtained, **BUT** those who were **chosen** obtained it, and the rest were hardened (Romans 11:7).

Scriptures dealing with the *elect* and the *chosen* consistently portray them as the redeemed Jewish and Gentile remnant Church and clearly distinguish them from literal Israel. It is to these elect, Jesus' disciples, that the warnings of Matthew 24 apply. It is not biblical to teach that these Scriptures do not apply to the present-day Church. Jesus' obvious intent is that these warnings be applied to the Churches throughout the age, for He provides warnings specifically applicable to His contemporaries as well as those elect/chosen who would be alive at the end of the age. His first warning to them was a warning to not be misled.

> And Jesus answered and said to them, "See to it that no one misleads you. For many will come in My name, saying, 'I am the Christ,' and will mislead many" (Matthew 24:4-5).

All believers who have ears to hear will find His words applicable to them. "See to it that no one misleads **YOU**." Who is it that has been led astray recently in direct fulfillment of this prophecy? Who is it that has followed false Christs to cultic deaths all over the world? Were they literal Jews, or were they contemporary believers of all nationalities being led astray by false teachers in the name of Christ?

Are Other Parts of Matthew also *Inapplicable* to the Church?

Jesus spent His public ministry teaching and demonstrating to His disciples how to carry on His work. The beatitudes and the parables and the great commission and all of His teachings were directed specifically to His disciples. Is there any teaching of Jesus to His disciples which does not apply to the Churches throughout the age?

Why should the present-day Church assume that the rest of the book of Matthew is applicable to them if Matthew 24 is not? Why have we assumed that the beatitudes and the great commission are applicable to the Church if Matthew 24 is not?

Some of our doctrine needs changing. We should start listening to what Jesus said. After Matthew 24 comes Matthew 25, and the Church takes it right up as applicable. Finally, in Matthew 28:16-20, after His resurrection and appearance to His disciples in Galilee, Jesus gives to His disciples, still Jews, the great commission to go into all the world and make disciples of all nations. And of course the Church has taken this, rightly so, as a word to the Church, even though the *YOU* to whom He was speaking is the same audience as the *YOU* to whom He was speaking in Matthew 24. Notice that in the context of the great commission, He said He would be with them **until the end of the age.**

We can't pick and choose Scriptures like that. **Disciples are disciples, whether they are Jew or Gentile and of one century or another.** These warnings to the disciples at Jerusalem are timeless and applicable to the entire Church age. Jesus was clearly addressing both His contemporaries and those who would be alive at the end of the age.

Jesus' First Warning: "Do not be Deceived!"

If we fall for this deception, we will have played into the hands of the enemy and ignored Jesus' most crucial end-time warnings. I pray that you sense the work of the deceiver in this. I pray that you see that this is exactly what the enemy of our souls would have us believe. Do not be led into this trap. The obvious spin-off of the Church not heeding these warnings will be great numbers stumbling and falling away when the truth becomes obvious. Do not let yourself be deceived!

> Then they will deliver **you** to tribulation, and will kill **you,** and **you** will be hated by all nations on account of My name. And at that time many will fall away and will deliver up one another and hate one another. And many false prophets will arise, and will mislead many. And because lawlessness is increased, most people's love will grow cold. But the one who endures to the end, he shall be saved (Matthew 24:9-13).

We are all called to follow Jesus, not to avoid the path He walked. The closer we study Scriptures relevant to the end of the age, the closer we see that the walk of the Church parallels the walk of Jesus. There is not one way for Him and another for us. The devil would like us to think so, but he is a liar and a deceiver. The devil says to lay down our crosses, and Jesus says to pick up our crosses and follow Him. Who will we listen to?

Whoever They are, They are Full of the Holy Spirit

The Olivet Discourse of Matthew 24 is also portrayed in Mark 13 and Luke 21. To get a fuller understanding of who the elect are in Matthew 24, we should look at all three gospel narratives, or we will be basing our conclusions on less information than what God has given us.

> For nation will arise against nation, and kingdom against kingdom; there will be earthquakes in various places; there will also be famines. These things are merely the beginning of birth pangs. But be on **your** guard; for they will deliver **you** to the courts, and **you** will be flogged in the synagogues, and **you** will stand before governors and kings for My sake, as a testimony to them. And the gospel must first be preached to all the nations. And when they arrest **you** and deliver **you** up, do not be anxious beforehand about what **you** are to say, but say whatever is given **you** in that hour; for it is not **you** who speak, but it is the Holy Spirit. And brother will deliver brother to death, and a father his child; and children will rise up against parents and have them put to death. And **you** will be hated by all on account of My name, **but the one who endures to the end, he shall be saved** (Mark 13:8-13).

Whoever it is that Jesus is talking to and calling *You* in this discourse and encouraging to endure to the end of the age, they are mouthpieces for the Holy Spirit. At the time Jesus was speaking, those who would be flogged in the synagogues would of course be His Jewish disciples who had changed their beliefs to incorporate Jesus as their Messiah, as there were yet no Gentiles in the Church. And they were full of the Holy Spirit. Jesus was Jewish and His first disciples were Jewish, but these words are applicable to His future disciples of all nations, tribes, peoples, and tongues.

Testimonies before governors and kings imply the preaching of the gospel to all nations. The commission to carry the gospel to all nations has been picked up by a Church which is largely Gentile, and it is clearly in context with the preaching of the gospel to all nations that this persecution will also apply. They will be hated by all nations on account of the name of Jesus Christ. Jesus' disciples, whether they are Jewish or Gentile, are called to endure to the end. The first Christians were hated on account of the name of Jesus Christ, and Christians today are also hated on account of the name of Jesus Christ, and Christians during the great tribulation will be more hated on account of the name of Jesus Christ. That hatred is intensifying daily and is obvious to anyone who is following the tribulations of the persecuted Church. These are wide-range prophecies which exclude none of the Church but incorporate His disciples throughout the age.

> If the world hates **you**, you know that it has hated Me before it hated **you**. If you were of the world, the world would love its own; but because you are not of the world, but I chose you out of the world, therefore the world hates **you** . . . These things I have spoken to **you,** that **you** may be kept from stumbling. They will make **you** outcasts from the synagogue, but an hour is coming for everyone who kills **you** to think that he is offering service to God. And these things they will do, because they have not known the Father, or Me. But these things I have spoken to **you,** that when their hour comes, **you** may remember that I told **you** of them (John 15:18-19, 16:1-4).

Notice that Jesus said, **"These things I have spoken to you, that you may be kept from stumbling."** We must understand that these warnings are to Jesus' followers, to His disciples, to you and me if we are His disciples. Jesus is warning us **so that we will not stumble when these things come!** It is potentially devastating to teach that these warnings are not applicable to the current Church. It is a setup from the pit of hell!

If Jesus gave these warnings to preclude His disciples from stumbling, and yet the present-day Church believes these warnings need not apply, they are treading on dangerous ground. Many **will** stumble and fall away — a great number of them — when they find themselves in tribulation they neither expect nor understand nor for which they are prepared. Sadly, that is what Jesus said would happen.

This is not a casual point of doctrinal discussion. It may be the issue that determines whether we as believers endure to the end or fall away. Notice how closely Jesus' prophetic words to His disciples were fulfilled in the persecution and martyrdom of Stephen, the first of His disciples to die for their faith and a model for the Church thereafter. Acts Chapters 6 and 7 prove that Jesus' words are directed to His Church. Everything that Jesus said His disciples should expect happened to Stephen.

The Proof of Applicability is Before Our Eyes

We need not speculate whether Matthew 24 applies or not to the present-day Church. Jesus' prophetic words to His disciples are being fulfilled in the persecutions and martyrdoms of Christians world-wide at this very moment and to an increasing degree. Any hesitancy in applying Matthew 24 to the present-day Church should fade away as we observe the persecution already falling. A well-known international ministry which deals with the persecuted Church recently reported that of the nominally two billion world-wide who claim to be Christian, two-thirds of that number were already, as of 1998, being persecuted or directly threatened with persecution. The numbers are growing, not lessening. Jesus' prophecies will come true. We in the Western Church may be able to bury our heads in the sand a little longer, but we will soon be forced to wake up. I just read a newsletter yesterday telling of a Chinese pastor in the house Church movement who is burning prosperity-doctrine literature supplied by the Western Church because it is inapplicable, and even worse, misleading.

How devastating it is that current Christian authors are still proclaiming that Matthew 24 does not apply to the present-day Church. The Chinese house Church movement is in serious tribulation now and has been for years! May God have mercy on us for not more properly warning them. The true Church has been in tribulation since it was birthed! But we're no threat to Satan with our lukewarm escapist teachings. No wonder he doesn't bother us!

Nate Krupp, the publisher of this book, relates that in 1976 Corrie ten Boom personally shared with him that the Chinese Christians had been taught a pre-tribulation rapture. When the Communist take-over came in 1949-50, many believers fell away. The Christian leaders of China confessed to Corrie ten Boom that they had taught their congregations wrongly and repented of their teaching. This testimony indicates that the pre-tribulation teaching has been evaluated in one of the world's largest harvest fields and has been found lacking. It does not witness to reality during times of persecution and becomes a stumbling stone to the saints who believe it.

The wisdom of men does not establish truth. Jesus is truth and what He said is truth. The hope of the Church is to escape God's wrath, not to escape all tribulation. Tribulation is designed to purify and refine us and make us worthy of the Kingdom of God. We should not seek to short-circuit the process designed to refine us into the likeness of Jesus. Yet we wail in our wombs, having swallowed Satan's lies, and rage against the thought of the very birth pangs that are intended to birth us into the sons of God for which all creation is waiting.

The problem with sheep is that they can easily be led astray. We have been sold a false expectation by the enemy of our souls. We are being fed from poisonous pastures of false doctrine. The Church is being set up for a great falling away because we do not understand, and we have no vision.

Reason or Revelation?

I was recently reading a book which was a compilation of various author's reasons why they believe in the pre-tribulation rapture. The passages used to defend the pre-tribulation position were the very same as others would use to defend other positions. This was discouraging. These were scholars with seminary degrees and knowledge of Greek and Hebrew. People are going to pay attention to them merely because of their credentials. We would be much better served by ignorant fisherman who know Jesus Christ.

Not all of us are Greek scholars able to follow, or interested in following, teachings that hang extensive doctrinal conclusions on the tense of a verb — or even worse — on arguments of silence. Somehow I don't think Peter and John were either. I have followed too many of these teachings which were based on motive rather than a search for truth. Refuting each point would take volumes. My spirit and mind both tell me it's all an intricate deception, but that's easy to say. Where's the proof that it's a deception? It's not going to be settled by compiling the opinions of men and making a list of all the points on one side versus those on the other and coming to a jury decision. That's not how truth is arrived at. Arguing along that line would just add fuel to a foolish fire. The truth will come to us by the only way truth can come, by revelation of the Scriptures brought to life by the Holy Spirit. The Holy Spirit will lead us into **all** truth.

Let the Holy Spirit Lead You

Matthew 24:13 reads, **"But the one who endures to the end, he shall be saved."** If I say that these are Jesus' words to His disciples alive at the end of the age, those of pre-tribulation position will insist otherwise. They will insist that this is speaking of the Jews or those who have come to faith during the tribulation, for the *true Church* has already been raptured out. Although that disturbs me, what can I say to you that would be of any use? I have tried to use logic. I have said something like, "Why, then, in all the rest of the book of Matthew, when Jesus is speaking to His disciples, is it assumed He is speaking to all of His disciples throughout the age? For instance, the great commission, the beatitudes, the parables, etc., are never considered as exclusively for the Jews but for His followers throughout the age. Why then is Matthew 24 held by pre-tribulation advocates as referring to Jews and not the Church? And where is the evidence of a prior rapture?" And we could argue back and forth. And where would that leave you? Don't believe me. Believe Jesus. Don't let a man interpret Jesus' words to you. Let the Holy Spirit do that. God will often speak through a man — but so will Satan — sometimes in the next breath. Peter demonstrated that for us.

The point of this is that in one way or another, Jesus is going to have to tell you whether the warnings of Matthew 24 are for you or not. The Holy Spirit must lead you into the truth of this. And it must be the Holy Spirit's voice that you hear, not the voice of the enemy. Jesus' first words to His disciple's questions regarding the end of the age were, **"See to it that no one misleads you."** Men will mislead you. The Holy Spirit will not. Get alone with Him and settle this thing the only way it can be settled, with revelation directly from Him. Let Him quicken to you whether these warnings of Jesus apply to you or not. We are far too used to listening to the teachings of men which are not in line with the teachings of the written word confirmed by the Holy Spirit.

"Father, once again I pray to bind the efforts of the enemy to deceive us in these critical areas. I pray that all who read these Scriptures yet one more time would be quickened by the Holy Spirit to the truth contained therein. I pray that our preferences and motives would not override the still small voice of conviction that applies these Scriptures as You would have them applied. Father, we desperately need Your wisdom and revelation to keep from being deceived. I ask this in the name of Jesus, Whose appearance we long for and Whose glory we seek in these days at the very end of the age. May Your wisdom be demonstrated through a Church who says 'Yes!' to Your plan for us on earth up until the time we are rescued from wrath."

SIX

A Theology of Suffering

> The Spirit Himself bears witness with our spirit that we are children of God, and if children, heirs also, heirs of God and fellow heirs with Christ, if indeed we suffer with Him in order that we may also be glorified with Him. For I consider that the sufferings of this present time are not worthy to be compared with the glory that is to be revealed to us. For the anxious longing of the creation waits eagerly for the revealing of the sons of God. For the creation was subjected to futility, not of its own will, but because of Him who subjected it, in hope that the creation itself also will be set free from its slavery to corruption into the freedom of the glory of the children of God. For we know that the whole creation groans and suffers the pains of childbirth together until now. And not only this, but also we ourselves, having the first fruits of the Spirit, even we ourselves groan within ourselves, waiting eagerly for our adoption as sons, the redemption of our body (Romans 8:16-23).

Because of corruption, God has subjected His creation to futility. But that is not the end of His plan. Out of futility comes redemption and transformation. The process is likened to a birthing. It was mentioned that a baby, given a choice, would probably not opt for the birthing process, even though that is the only path that leads to life. Pressure, discomfort, and being kicked out of a warm and comfortable place are initiations into this *transformation/birthing* process.

It is no accident that Jesus likened the events at the end of this age to birth pains. Wars, famines, and plagues are not our idea of transforming processes, but they are servants in God's plan to restore His fallen creation to glory. And if the wars, rumors of wars, famines, and earthquakes of Matthew 24:8 are merely the beginning of birth pangs, will not the delivering to tribulation and the killing of the disciples described immediately following in Matthew 24:9 be more advanced labor pains? And will not the object of all of these labor pains be a birth?

> "Shall I bring to the point of birth, and not give delivery?" says the LORD. "Or shall I who gives delivery shut the womb?" says your God (Isaiah 66:9).

And will not that birth be the birth of the sons of God for which all of creation eagerly awaits while groaning in the pains of childbirth?

The Redemptive Nature of Suffering

The above Scriptures indicate that God has set things up so that the suffering of His creation is redemptive. The whole creation is said to be groaning as in the pains of childbirth, straining toward the purposes for which God has designed it. It is not just the elect/chosen of creation who suffer redemptively; the whole creation suffers redemptively. The judgments of God are clearly redemptive up to and including the outpouring of the sixth bowl of Revelation 16:15.

How can the terrifying judgments and wrath of the trumpets and bowls be redemptive judgments from the hand of a loving God? Because at the sixth trumpet, the fourth bowl, and the fifth bowl are found the words **"and they did not repent."** God's judgments, even up until the seventh bowl, are therefore clearly redemptive, for God has continued to leave open the door of repentance up until the last minute. God has answered the prayer of Habakkuk.

> LORD, I have heard the report about Thee and I fear. O LORD, revive Thy work in the midst of the years, in the midst of the years make it known; in wrath remember mercy (Habakkuk 3:2).

All judgments of God up to the last bowl of wrath are redemptive, for He is long-suffering and not willing that any should perish. In wrath, He **has** remembered mercy.

> ... for when the earth experiences Thy judgments the inhabitants of the world learn righteousness (Isaiah 26:9).

However, God will not contend with man forever. There is a terrible and final day of judgment awaiting those who do not repent. Sodom and Gomorrah are witnesses of that. And even the final judgment is redemptive in that creation is at last purged of unredeemable evil.

> Just as Sodom and Gomorrah and the cities around them, since they in the same way as these indulged in gross immorality and went after strange flesh, are exhibited as an example, in undergoing the punishment of eternal fire (Jude 1:7).

I believe Scripture indicates the judgment of Sodom and Gomorrah matches the final judgment of the seventh bowl. Up until that point, God's wrath is tempered and mixed with mercy. Up until that point, there continues to be an offer of salvation through repentance. Beyond that point, there is no longer an offer of repentance. Every last soul to be saved has been wrung from the earth, and the remnant is doomed to fiery destruction, having turned away from His final offer of salvation.

The staggering description of the severity of God's judgments up until the seventh bowl, still redemptive in nature, should give us some inkling of the horror and reality of what is reserved for those who choose to turn away from the living God. Indeed, it would have been better for these if they had never been born. The terrors of the trumpet and bowl judgments are merely the kindness of God relative to the horror which awaits those who do not repent.

> Behold then the kindness and severity of God . . . (Romans 11:22).

Perhaps with this sobering perspective, we can now begin to understand that the sufferings of creation, up until the time of final judgment, are redemptive. There will be wrath without mercy for those who ultimately choose not to repent, but the clear intent of the seals, trumpets, and bowls is to lead men to repentance. We have been too quick to prescribe wrath without mercy to the seals, trumpets, and bowl judgments. Consequently, we tend to remove the Church from amidst them, for we know that the Church is not appointed to wrath. But she is appointed to judgment and tribulation.

Tribulation or Wrath?

It is a huge mistake to confuse wrath and tribulation and to mistakenly ascribe one to the other. For instance, if we ascribe wrath to the final seven years of the age and then find ourselves amidst it, our faith will be shaken. We need to correctly distinguish between wrath and tribulation so that we do not find ourselves entering tribulation thinking it is wrath.

The problem lies in our lack of understanding of the differences in purpose between tribulation and wrath and evidences our lack of understanding of the way of the cross to which we are called. Jesus said that on earth we would have tribulation, but that we are not appointed to wrath. Tribulation and wrath are mutually exclusive in nature and of vastly different intents.

Scripture indicates that God uses Satan's fury toward mankind both in tribulation and in wrath. The degree of Satan's fury that God allows to be released in tribulation of the saints is much less than what He allows to be released in wrath against the unrepentant world. I read somewhere that

Satan is like an angry dog tethered on a rope. He is only allowed as much rope as God gives him. The story of Job comes to mind. Satan is not in charge. He is God's devil!

Tribulation is God's loving and disciplinary provision to form us into the image of His Son. Wrath is His judgment on an unbelieving and unrepentant world. This is clearly pointed out by Paul to the Thessalonians when he said that although they have been destined for affliction (1 Thessalonians 3:3), they are not destined for wrath (1 Thessalonians 5:9). He explained that the very purpose of persecution and affliction was to make them worthy for the Kingdom of God (2 Thessalonians 1:5). That's about as clear as it can get.

Persecutions and Afflictions Make Us Worthy . . .

> Grace to you and peace from God the Father and the Lord Jesus Christ. We ought always to give thanks to God for you, brethren, as is only fitting, because your faith is greatly enlarged, and the love of each one of you toward one another grows ever greater; therefore, we ourselves speak proudly of you among the churches of God for your perseverance and faith in the midst of all your persecutions and afflictions which you endure. This is a plain indication of God's righteous judgment **so that you may be considered worthy of the kingdom of God, for which indeed you are suffering** (2 Thessalonians 1:2-5).

Have we ever considered that our persecutions and afflictions make us worthy of the Kingdom of God? That's what the Bible says. They are literally then more precious than gold.

I confess that I write this better than I live it. May the Lord establish it in my heart as well as my head. May He do the same for you.

> In this you greatly rejoice, even though now for a little while, **if necessary,** you have been distressed by various trials, that the proof of your faith, being more precious than gold which is perishable, even though tested by fire,

may be found to result in praise and glory and honor at the revelation of Jesus Christ . . . (1 Peter 1:6-7).

Consider it all joy, my brethren, when you encounter various trials, knowing that the testing of your faith produces endurance. And let endurance have its perfect result, that you may be perfect and complete, lacking in nothing (James 1:2-4).

For it was fitting for Him, for whom are all things, and through whom are all things, in bringing many sons to glory, to perfect the author of their salvation through sufferings (Hebrews 2:10).

If persecution and affliction are designed to make us worthy for the Kingdom of God, we need to eagerly take that medicine, even though the initial taste may be bitter. Teachings that the final seven years of the age are God's wrath are setting the Church up for a shaking when the Church realizes that she has entered the final seven years of the age unraptured. How encouraging will be the explanation that this is a time of refining and testing to make one worthy of the Kingdom of God.

For it is time for **judgment** to begin with the household of God; and if it begins with us first, what will be the outcome for those who do not obey the gospel of God (1 Peter 4:17)?

Beloved, do not be surprised at the **fiery ordeal** among you, which comes upon you for your testing, as though some strange thing were happening to you; but to the degree that you share the **sufferings** of Christ, keep on rejoicing; so that also at the revelation of His glory, you may rejoice with exultation (1 Peter 4:12-13).

And after you have **suffered** for a little while, the God of all grace, who called you to His eternal glory in Christ, will Himself perfect, confirm, strengthen and establish you (1 Peter 5:10).

. . . so that no man may be disturbed by these **afflictions;** for you yourselves know that we have been destined for this. For indeed when we were with you, we kept telling you in advance that we were going to **suffer affliction;** and so it came to pass, as you know (1 Thessalonians 3:3-4).

For this finds favor, if for the sake of conscience toward God a man bears up under sorrows when **suffering** unjustly. For what credit is there if, when you sin and are harshly treated, you endure it with patience? But if when you do what is right and **suffer** for it you patiently endure it, this finds favor with God. For you have been called for this purpose, since Christ also suffered for you, leaving you an example for you to follow in His steps . . . (1 Peter 2:19-21).

For it is better, if God should will it so, that you **suffer** for doing what is right rather than for doing what is wrong (1 Peter 3:17).

Therefore, since Christ has suffered in the flesh, arm yourselves also with the **same purpose** . . . (1 Peter 4:1).

Purged, Purified, and Refined

God disciplines those He loves. The purpose of our tribulations is to make us worthy of the Kingdom of God.

And some of those who have insight will fall, in order to refine, purge, and make them pure, until the end time; because it is still to come at the appointed time (Daniel 11:35).

And he said, "Go your way, Daniel, for these words are concealed and sealed up until the end time. Many will be purged, purified and refined; but the wicked will act wickedly, and none of the wicked will understand, but those who have insight will understand" (Daniel 12:9-10).

And I gave her time to repent; and she does not want to repent of her immorality. Behold, I will cast her upon a bed of sickness, and those who commit adultery with her into great tribulation, unless they repent of her deeds. And I will kill her children with pestilence; and **all the churches will know** that I am He who searches the minds and hearts; and **I will give to each one of you according to your deeds** (Revelation 2:21-23).

A solemn message to each of us is contained here. There is a destiny undeniably referred to as "great tribulation" into which it is possible to be cast. And by observation, **all the Churches will know** during this time of great tribulation that Jesus gives to each one according to one's deeds.

This is a sobering thought which implies that the Churches will be on earth during this time of testing. The nature of our deeds, our unrepented and perhaps even unaware individual sins, determine what we will receive during this time. This sounds much like the Scriptures of Daniel in which many will be purged, purified and refined for the purposes of making them pure. Isn't this the purity that Jesus is seeking in His bride?

> ... that He might present to Himself the church in all her glory, having no spot or wrinkle or any such thing; but that she should be holy and blameless (Ephesians 5:27).

Peter had to stumble so that he could be purged, purified and refined. He was the one who would never deny Jesus, even though the others might. But Peter did not know his own heart even as we do not know our own hearts. Sober reflection on the process that Peter had to be taken through should prepare us for whatever it takes to refine us into the Bride of Christ. Notice that Jesus prayed that Peter's faith would not fail, but He did not pray that Peter would not stumble. For Peter had to stumble in order to be purged, purified and refined. And it was only then that Jesus could say to him, "Feed my sheep."

> "Simon, Simon, behold, Satan has demanded permission to sift you like wheat; but I have prayed for you, that your faith may not fail; and you, when once you have turned again, strengthen your brothers." And he said to Him, "Lord, with You I am ready to go both to

prison and to death!" And He said, "I say to you, Peter, the cock will not crow today until you have denied three times that you know Me" (Luke 22:31-34).

We know how this happened and how, when the cock crowed, Peter went out and "wept bitterly." Peter experienced the cross. To the extent we have not yet experienced the cross in the details of our lives, so will we find ourselves eventually in situations of stumbling and bitter weeping. The cross must be applied to all the details of our lives for how else will we be purified? We can take our medicine now or we can take it later. God will not be mocked. We will receive as we have sown. And all the Churches will know that our individual hearts and minds are searched and that we are given according to our deeds.

Notice that Satan **demanded** permission, as if he had a right to sift Peter. And indeed he did, for sin in our lives allows Satan's access, but not without redemptive purposes. Jesus will have His glorious Church in spite of our kicking and squealing. We need to grow up and embrace this birthing process instead of fighting against it. Pray that we might gain insight and vision in order to not fall away.

And They Overcame Him

> And the God of peace will soon crush Satan under your feet (Romans 16:20).

> And I heard a loud voice in heaven, saying, "Now the salvation, and the power, and the kingdom of our God and the authority of His Christ have come, for the accuser of our brethren has been thrown down, who accuses them before our God day and night. And **they overcame him** because of the blood of the Lamb and because of the word of their testimony, and they did not love their life even to death" (Revelation 12:10-11).

Here we see the purposes for the suffering of the Church. It is the price we agree to pay in order to overcome Satan. Did we think that Jesus already paid the price so we wouldn't have to suffer? No, Jesus paid the price so that the Church **could** suffer in His power and authority, and thus overcome Satan thereby demonstrating God's wisdom **through her** to the rulers and authorities in the heavenly places. This is the purpose for the suffering of the Church. Are we willing to pay the price that Paul paid?

> ... he is a chosen instrument of Mine, to bear My name before the Gentiles and kings and the sons of Israel; for I will show him how much he must suffer for My name's sake (Acts 9:15-16).

Were Paul's sufferings redemptive? Our own salvation may well attest to it. The salvation of others may one day attest to our willingness as well to suffer so as to fill up the sufferings lacking in the Body of Christ.

> Now I rejoice in my sufferings for your sake, and in my flesh I do my share on behalf of His body (which is the church) in filling up that which is lacking in Christ's afflictions (Colossians 1:24).

If Paul had a share of suffering to fulfill, we all have a share to fulfill. With a greater call to suffering comes a greater grace to endure. So it will be at the end of the age when the extent of suffering will be exceeded only by the grace to endure. When Jesus said "It is finished," He had accomplished everything that He had come to do. He had gained the victory over Satan. The provision of gaining this victory is that He has the legal authority to delegate to His Church on earth whatever yet remains to be done in the eternal purpose of God to demonstrate His wisdom through the Church. It is His choice. If He has decided that additional worldly suffering is needed to fill up what He considers lacking in His affliction, so be it. There is nothing the Church has to offer in this but her consent. We can be at best empty and cleansed vessels through which He can demonstrate His life and His death.

> Now I rejoice in my sufferings for your sake ...

We glorify God by rejoicing in our sufferings.

> So they went on their way from the presence of the Council, rejoicing that they had been considered worthy to suffer shame for His name (Acts 5:41).

> Rejoice in the Lord always; again I will say, rejoice! Let your forbearing spirit be known to all men. The Lord is near. Be anxious for nothing, but in everything by prayer and supplication with thanksgiving let your requests be made known to God. And the peace of God, which surpasses all comprehension, shall guard your hearts and your minds in Christ Jesus (Philippians 4:4-7).

The mystery of the wisdom of the cross will be demonstrated by a Church who lives the beatitudes rather than just recites them. God will be glorified, and Satan will be crushed underfoot.

Stephen as a Model of the Last-day Saint . . . A Call to Martyrdom

> . . . and they chose Stephen, a man full of faith and of the Holy Spirit . . . (Acts 6:5).

Stephen was chosen to wait on tables. Perhaps we would expect and prefer to be at podiums in front of thousands, but Stephen, a man full of faith and of the Holy Spirit, was chosen to wait on tables. He was in obedience and position to fulfill that perfect work which God had chosen for him before time began.

We have seen how Stephen's martyrdom follows the prophetic pattern Jesus taught His disciples on the Mount of Olives. Stephen was falsely accused and brought before the council where he was given utterance and wisdom which none of his opponents could refute. It was not Stephen speaking; it was the Holy Spirit. It was the opportunity for his testimony. He was hated on account of Jesus' name, and he was put to death. And yet not a hair of his head perished. This is exactly what Jesus said His disciples should expect. This should be our expectation of the typical rather than the unusual.

> Truly, truly, I say to you, unless a grain of wheat falls into the earth and dies, it remains by itself alone; but if it dies, it bears much fruit. He who loves his life loses it; and he who hates his life in this world shall keep it to life eternal. If anyone serves Me, let him follow Me; and where I am, there shall My servant also be; if anyone serves Me, the Father will honor him (John 12:24-26).

> And they overcame him because of the blood of the Lamb and because of the word of their testimony, and they did not love their life even to death (Revelation 12:11).

> Here is the perseverance of the saints who keep the commandments of God and their faith in Jesus. And I heard a voice from heaven, saying, "Write, 'Blessed are the dead who die in the Lord from now on!'" (Revelation 14:12-13).

Our heels will be bruised, but we will bruise the serpent's head. We will overcome spiritually by allowing ourselves to be overcome physically. Satan will make the same fatal mistake of killing the saints that he made by putting Jesus on the cross.

Laying down our lives is for a redemptive purpose. A seed brings forth a hundred-fold as it falls to the ground and dies. We are called to offer ourselves as living sacrifices, as sheep to be slaughtered. For precious in God's sight is the death of His saints. Clinging to our lives will cause us to lose them; laying our lives down will allow us to gain them. In this manner the Church will crush Satan underfoot. We must begin absorbing these truths of God, rather than the things of men, and begin moving toward this glorious destiny.

Jews and Gentiles and Redemptive Suffering

The seeming paradox of the wisdom of the cross advises us to voluntarily lay down our lives for the sake of others. There is also an involuntary loss of one's life for God's higher purposes which is clearly redemptive. In the curious history of the Jew and the Gentile, we have seen some of each. At the end of the age, we will witness the ultimate demonstration of redemptive suffering as Jew and Gentile alike will be privileged to lay down their lives for the sake of each other. We have not yet seen the final holocaust, either Jewish or Christian.

> Then I heard the voice of the Lord, saying, "Whom shall I send, and who will go for Us?" Then I said, "Here am I. Send me!" And He said, "Go, and tell this people: 'Keep on listening, but do not perceive; keep on looking, but do not understand.' Render the hearts of this people insensitive, their ears dull, and their eyes dim, lest they see with their eyes, hear with their ears, understand with their hearts, and return and be healed." Then I said, "Lord, how long?" And He answered, "**Until** cities are devastated and without inhabitant, houses are without people, and the land is utterly desolate, the LORD has removed men far away, and the forsaken places are many in the midst of the land" (Isaiah 6:8-12).

It may be tempting to consider that this *until* has been historically accomplished. But has Israel returned to their God? The answer is no. Israel will remain partially blinded by the Hand of God until the fullness of the Gentiles has come in.

> What then? That which Israel is seeking for, it has not obtained, but those who were chosen obtained it, and the rest were hardened; just as it is written, "God gave them a spirit of stupor, eyes to see not and ears to hear not, down to this very day" (Romans 11:7-8).

> I say then, they did not stumble so as to fall, did they? May it never be! But by their transgression salvation has come to the Gentiles, to make them jealous. Now if their transgression be riches for the world and their failure be riches for the Gentiles, how much more will their fulfillment be (Romans 11:11-12)!

> For just as you once were disobedient to God, but now have been shown mercy because of their disobedience, so these also now have been disobedient, in order that because of the mercy shown to you they also may now be shown mercy. For God has shut up all in disobedience that He might show mercy to all (Romans 11:30-32).

Israel as Suffering Servant

> **JUST AS** many were astonished at you, My people, so His appearance was marred more than any man, and His form more than the sons of men (Isaiah 52:14).

Just as indicates a commonality between the nation as suffering servant and Jesus as the suffering servant of Isaiah Chapter 53. Debates have gone on for millennia between Jew and Gentile as to whether Isaiah 53 refers to Jesus the Messiah or Israel the nation. The plain wording of Scripture indicates that both considerations are in view.

Paul develops the foundational nature of Israel in Romans 11 and calls Gentile believers not to be arrogant toward Jews who were as branches broken off for unbelief for the very purpose that the fullness of Gentiles could come in.

> Do not be arrogant toward the branches; but if you are arrogant, remember that it is not you who supports the root, but the root supports you (Romans 11:18).

> For I do not want you, brethren, to be uninformed of this mystery, lest you be wise in your own estimation, that a partial hardening has happened to Israel until the fullness of the Gentiles has come in . . . (Romans 11:25).

What is the extent of the debt of gratitude Gentiles owe their Jewish brethren for the price they have paid in history to see the fullness of the Gentiles come in?

Do we fully understand that one people has been blinded in part so that another people could see? A review of Jewish history reveals the price of suffering that this people has paid so that the Gentiles could receive God's mercy. Neither the Church nor Israel has been able to adequately grasp understanding of this, because it involves such considerations as the holocaust. Our minds are not able to associate such calamity with a loving God Who would allow His own chosen people to go through such distress, to some extent for the sake of the Gentiles.

We must remember that God is first of all judging Israel for their sin. That judgment stands by itself without Gentile consideration. But God works all things according to His purposes and uses the judgment of Israel for the benefit of the Gentiles. He is both kind and severe. Can we receive that Scripture says He has bound all over to disobedience so that He can have mercy on all?

> . . . in order that in the ages to come He might show the surpassing riches of His grace in kindness toward us in Christ Jesus (Ephesians 2:7).

> As an example, brethren, of suffering and patience, take the prophets who spoke in the name of the Lord. Behold, we count those blessed who have endured. You have heard of the endurance of Job and have seen the outcome of the Lord's dealings, that the Lord is full of compassion and is merciful (James 5:10-11).

Would we consider Job, sitting in the ashes scraping his head-to-foot sores with a piece of broken pottery, having lost all family and possessions except his nagging wife, an object of God's mercy and compassion? If this happened to us, would we lose ourselves in the misery of it all and consider that God had forsaken us? Have we really processed the story of Job? Job's condition in the ashes was part of the plan of God to demonstrate His compassion and mercy to Job, not just for the rest of his earthly life, but for eternity. We have a tendency to get caught up in the interim details, because we can't see the overall picture. God's compassion and mercy toward each of us is no less than toward Job. In the interim, however, God wants to demonstrate His wisdom through us to the rulers and authorities in the heavenly places. And this is going to require some suffering, redemptive though it may be.

Our inability to theologically process the past holocaust certainly renders us unable to theologically process the prophesied future holocausts. We are stumbling around in the dark when it comes to understanding the ways of our God. His thoughts are above our thoughts. His ways are above our ways. We are caught up with the significance of this world and our lives in it, and we are unable to evaluate the relative insignificance of our present earthly lives in light of the eternal glory that is promised to those who endure.

God's Love Amidst Slaughter?

> Who shall separate us from the love of Christ? Shall tribulation, or distress, or persecution, or famine, or nakedness, or peril, or sword? Just as it is written, "For Thy sake we are being put to death all day long; we were considered as sheep to be slaughtered." But in all these things we overwhelmingly conquer through Him who loved us. For I am convinced that neither death, nor life, nor angels, nor principalities, nor things present, nor things to come, nor powers, nor height, nor depth, nor any other created thing, shall be able to separate us from the love of God, which is in Christ Jesus our Lord (Romans 8:35-39).

The book of Revelation has been described as a love letter to the Church, because it is a book about overcoming sin and of being conformed to the likeness of Jesus. Many saints do not see it that way. Much of the book is so offensive to the natural mind that the Church is written out of it. Most might have difficulty in ascribing the events of the fourth and fifth seals to God's love. The pale rider of the fourth seal and his companion are given authority over one-fourth of the earth's population to kill as they choose. The description of the martyrs of the fifth seal, who have lost their lives because of the word of God and their testimony, suggests that this one-fourth of the world may be largely Christians. And yet they are told to wait a little longer until the full number of their brethren and fellow servants are likewise killed. Apparently one-fourth of the earth is not yet sufficient. Can this be the love of God?

Was the cross of Christ the love of God? You won't be able to answer the first question unless you can answer this one. Jesus endured the agony and death of the cross for the joy set before Him. Is our call any different from His? The lives of those who choose to follow Jesus closely will most closely parallel His life.

> If the world hates you, you know that it has hated Me before it hated you. If you were of the world, the world would love its own; but because you are not of the world, but I chose you out of the world, therefore the world hates you. Remember the word that I said to you, "A slave is not greater than his master." If they persecuted Me, they will also persecute you; if they kept My word, they will keep yours also . . . These things I have spoken to you, that you may be kept from stumbling. They will make you outcasts from the synagogue, but an hour is coming for everyone who kills you to think that he is offering service to God. And these things they will do, because they have not known the Father, or Me. But these things I have spoken to you, that when their hour comes, you may remember that I told you of them . . . These things I have spoken to you, that in Me you may have peace. In the world you have tribulation, but take courage; I have overcome the world (John 15:18-20, 16:1-4, 33).

We must see **all** that comes into our lives as God's dealings with each of us with the intent of conforming each of us to the likeness of His Son. If we do not, we will be unable to endure that which we are called to endure. We must understand that the end of the age will be a birthing process, not painless, resulting in our ultimate births as the sons of God. We must understand that **NOTHING** will touch us except by the loving hand of our Father with this focused intent. If we do not see this, our faith will be shaken in the times of trouble ahead, and we will be tempted to fall away, not trusting and understanding a God Who would bring such things to bear on His children. It will indeed be God's love, although perhaps not our short-term sentimental view of it.

> They were stoned, they were sawn in two, they were tempted, they were put to death with the sword; they went about in sheepskins, in goatskins, being destitute, afflicted, ill-treated (men of whom the world was not worthy), wandering in deserts and mountains and caves and holes in the ground. And all these, having gained approval through their faith, did not receive what was promised, because God had provided something better for us, so that apart from us they should not be made perfect. Therefore, since we have so great a cloud of witnesses surrounding us, let us also lay aside every encumbrance, and the sin which so easily entangles us,

and let us run with endurance the race that is set before us, fixing our eyes on Jesus, the author and perfecter of faith, who for the joy set before Him endured the cross, despising the shame, and has sat down at the right hand of the throne of God. For consider Him who has endured such hostility by sinners against Himself, so that you may not grow weary and lose heart (Hebrews 11:37-12:3).

A Christian Holocaust?

Can we theologically appropriate a Christian holocaust when we have not yet appropriated a Jewish one? Have we appropriated the holocaust of Jesus? We don't know as we ought to know. There is ample scriptural evidence, though we may not eagerly embrace it, that the end of this age will be a time of virtual slaughter of Christians who refuse to bow down to the antichrist system. This will not be a mindless waste of life any more than Jesus' death was a mindless waste of life. We are as sheep to be slaughtered, seed to be sown, and drink offerings to be poured out. That "they loved not their lives unto death" is one of the acts of witness that overcome Satan at the end of this age by those who believe in Jesus. Precious in the eyes of God is the death of His saints. Redemptive is the death of His saints in demonstrating His wisdom to the rulers and authorities in the heavenly places.

Any unrest regarding this destiny should fade as the eternal realities of future glory overwhelm the transient realities of our earthly lives. We must see the joy set before us. We must develop eternal perspectives. This world and our physical lives need to fade away in terms of importance, and the sense of eternity needs to become our focus. We must see our treasures in heaven rather than on earth. If we don't change our world-views to heavenly views, how will we endure and overcome what lies ahead? Jesus, for the joy set before Him, endured the cross. Will we have any likelihood of enduring if we do not see the joy set before us? Pray that God would give us heavenly and eternal perspectives. Pray that we will indeed stand during these times. Pray that by the grace of God we will be brought to full stature as sons of God through these times of testing which are our destiny.

God has said that His Church is not appointed to His wrath. God is trustworthy. But it is clear from Scripture that the Church will be subject to Satan's fury for the ultimate purposes of crushing him underfoot and shaping us into the likeness of Jesus. God isn't going to miss any assignments in this process. He's not going to give to you what should have gone to me. God's touch in each of our lives will be perfect, as it has been perfect up to this point. We need to get it settled in our minds and hearts and spirits that whatever comes to us in this life comes from the hand of God. Satan may sometimes be used as the postman, but God decides what is to be delivered. His deliveries are always perfect and precisely on time. Have you gotten to the point in your Christian walk where you have offered yourself as a living sacrifice, content and at rest as a chick under the wings of a mother hen?

We can grumble as the Israelites did in the desert, or we can settle the issue once and for all. We can decide to totally abandon ourselves to a Father Who has never failed to be trustworthy or deal perfectly for even a micro-second in the lives of one of His children. We need to reread Psalm 91. Let's resolve to give God the trust He so eagerly longs for and so fully deserves. Let us seek to please Him and glorify Him by our trust.

The Mind-set of Job

God delights in the trust of His saints. The displeasing behavior of the Israelites in the desert is recorded for us so that we do not repeat their mistakes of unbelief. And yet I find myself wavering and often absent of the joy of full trust and rest. And I have yet to go one day in the desert without water. God will find that in each of our lives which requires testing in order to reveal our hearts. Our testings will be individually tailored to *bring out the worst* to allow opportunity to repent and get rid of it and bring in the best.

Have any of us been tested as Job was? And yet it was Job who uttered the standard of trust,

> Though he slay me, yet will I trust in him . . . (Job 13:15 KJV).

So must we trust in God as we come to the end of this age. The explicit destiny of many of us in the Church is martyrdom. We must resolve beforehand the issue of whether God is or is not worthy of our trust. Although our resolve may not always be reflected by our daily performance, His record of trustworthiness, nevertheless, in every second of life of each one of His saints, is perfect. With this testimony of trustworthiness and with His word that He will never leave or forsake us, can we settle once and for all the issue of trusting implicitly in our loving heavenly Father, no matter what lies ahead for us and our loved ones? Can we agree to praise Him no matter what, knowing that everything coming from His loving hand is destined to aid in transforming us into the likeness of His perfect Son for eternity?

"Father, I pray for the grace to glorify You with the trust of Job. May we not displease You by shrinking back in times of testing."

Job is an end-time message to the Church. God elected to demonstrate His wisdom through Job to the rulers and authorities in the heavenly places, even as He will demonstrate His wisdom through the Church at the end of the age. The Church needs to come to grips with the fact that God's wisdom was not primarily demonstrated during the abundant times of Job's life, but during times of testing. The response of Job amidst that testing needs to be our response, for we have even more insight into the faithfulness of God. And it was God Who started it. He said to Satan, "Have you considered My servant Job?" God desired to demonstrate His wisdom to Satan through Job, and He desires to demonstrate His wisdom to Satan through the Church.

Do you think that in eternity Job will look back on his time of testing and consider that it was not the love of God?

Do you think Job will question whether or not God had his best interests in mind? Do you think Job would go back, if he could, and change one thing? Or do you think Job will acknowledge rather the perfect dealings of a loving Father Who dispenses perfectly in timing and degree?

I confess there is too much lag time between when a trial comes into my life and when I finally acknowledge it to be worth more than gold. My flesh would much rather be pampered than tested by adversity. But the road of transformation is a road necessarily mined with perfect adversities chosen individually by our Loving Father to put the flesh to death and to transform us into the likeness of Jesus.

"Thank You, Father, for the testimony of Job. May we all be found with the faith of Job when we stand before You."

Beauty for Ashes

God establishes perfection to His glory out of the very substance of our weakness and failure. God chooses to bring life forth out of death. Out of the seemingly unrecoverable God-forsaken ruins of the literal ashes of the Jewish holocaust will arise a resurrected people. Those chosen since before time began to be redeemed by the Blood of His Son will rise from their graves to once again live and play and grow old in the streets of Jerusalem. God's purposes are never thwarted. His promises and callings are never overruled or revoked. His original purposes for His chosen nation of Israel to be the source of sons for the world were not thwarted by their apostasy. Even their disobedience is redeemable. It was part of His plan from the beginning.

> As the pregnant woman approaches the time to give birth, she writhes and cries out in her labor pains, thus were we before Thee, O LORD. We were pregnant, we writhed in labor, we gave birth, as it were, only to wind. We could not accomplish deliverance for the earth nor were inhabitants of the world born (Isaiah 26:17-18).

This is Israel speaking. It is God Who now begins speaking through the prophet:

> Your dead will live; their corpses will rise. You who lie in the dust, awake and shout for joy, for your dew is as the dew of the dawn, and the earth will give birth to the departed spirits (Isaiah 26:19).

> Therefore prophesy, and say to them, "Thus says the Lord GOD, 'Behold, I will open your graves and cause you to come up out of your graves, My people; and I will bring you into the land of Israel. Then you will know that I am the LORD, when I have opened your graves and caused you to come up out of your graves, My people. And I will put My Spirit within you, and you will come to life, and I will place you on your own land. Then you will know that I, the LORD, have spoken and done it, declares the LORD'" (Ezekiel 37:12-14).

Israel will be resurrected, and she will see the fruits of her labor . . .

> Then you will say in your heart, "Who has begotten these for me, since I have been bereaved of my children, and am barren, an exile and a wanderer? And who has reared these? Behold, I was left alone; from where did these come?" (Isaiah 49:21).

> "Shout for joy, O barren one, you who have borne no child; break forth into joyful shouting and cry aloud, you who have not travailed; for the sons of the desolate one will be more numerous than the sons of the married woman," says the LORD (Isaiah 54:1).

> Now, why do you cry out loudly? Is there no king among you, or has your counselor perished, that agony has gripped you like a woman in childbirth? Writhe and labor to give birth, Daughter of Zion, like a woman in childbirth . . . (Micah 4:9-10).

> But as for you, Bethlehem Ephrathah, too little to be among the clans of Judah, from you One will go forth for Me to be ruler in Israel. His goings forth are from long ago, from the days of eternity. Therefore, He will give

them up until the time when she who is in labor has borne a child. Then the remainder of His brethren will return to the sons of Israel. And He will arise and shepherd His flock in the strength of the LORD, in the majesty of the name of the LORD His God. And they will remain, because at that time He will be great to the ends of the earth. And this One will be our peace (Micah 5:2-5).

For Zion's sake I will not keep silent, and for Jerusalem's sake I will not keep quiet, until her righteousness goes forth like brightness, and her salvation like a torch that is burning. And the nations will see your righteousness, and all kings your glory; and you will be called by a new name, which the mouth of the LORD will designate. You will also be a crown of beauty in the hand of the LORD, and a royal diadem in the hand of your God. It will no longer be said to you, "Forsaken," nor to your land will it any longer be said, "Desolate"; but you will be called, "My delight is in her," and your land, "Married"; for the LORD delights in you, and to Him your land will be married. For as a young man marries a virgin, so your sons will marry you; and as the bridegroom rejoices over the bride, so your God will rejoice over you. On your walls, O Jerusalem, I have appointed watchmen; all day and all night they will never keep silent. You who remind the LORD, take no rest for yourselves; and give Him no rest until He establishes and makes Jerusalem a praise in the earth (Isaiah 62:1-7).

All nations will then know that He is God and that He has done this thing. The question of, "How could a loving God allow Auschwitz?" will be forever silenced. Valleys of dry bones and ash heaps will spring to life in the twinkling of an eye. His justice and righteousness will be a banner for all nations. All nations will stand in awe at the majesty and power of the Living God. How His heart must yearn for that day when the price His Son paid will be reimbursed, and the Lamb will have gained His reward.

"Hallelujah!! Come quickly, Lord Jesus! Blessed is the One Who comes in the name of the Lord."

Let us choose to please Him now with our trust and praise and thanksgiving for the glory He is about to bring upon the earth.

SEVEN

Restoring the Stolen Vision

Astonishing Parallels

I began sensing some years ago that the Church's walk on earth during the last three and one-half years of this age would mirror Jesus' public ministry of three and one-half years. I remember studying Revelation and all the references to the last three and one-half years of the age, and I remember how my spirit leaped as I was walking along one day listening to a cassette tape and heard mention of Jesus' public ministry of three and one-half years. It was as if the Holy Spirit welded the two periods together in my mind, never again to be separated. It was one of those moments when you know God has spoken.

As we consider the public ministry of Jesus and compare it to the prophetic destiny of the Church outlined by Scripture for the last three and one-half years of the age, astonishing parallels emerge. We have seen that Ephesians 3:8-12 states that God created all things in order to demonstrate His wisdom through the Church to the rulers and authorities in the heavenly places. The wisdom of God is defined as the cross of Christ (1 Corinthians 1:24). We could then say that God will demonstrate the wisdom of the cross of Christ through the Church to the rulers and authorities in the heavenly places. The wisdom of the cross that God demonstrated through His Son will again be demonstrated through His Son's corporate body, the Church.

We have seen in Revelation 13:7 that Satan is allowed to war against the saints for three and one-half years and is granted authority to overcome them. It is no coincidence that both Jesus' time of public ministry and this particular period of time in which the saints are overcome/overcomers are both periods of three and one-half years. It is no coincidence that both Jesus and these saints are physically overcome at the end of these respective periods of three and one-half years and yet emerge victorious. That is the wisdom of the cross that God has chosen to demonstrate through His Son in both His individual and corporate form.

Revelation 12:9-10 describes a series of events that seem to occur simultaneously at the beginning of the final three and one-half years. Satan is thrown out of heaven to earth, and concurrently come the salvation, the power, the Kingdom of God, and the authority of Christ. Where will these things come other than to the saints alive on the earth at that time? This would seem to explain the source of the holiness and power of the saints of Daniel 12:7. It is coincident with the giving of authority to the two witnesses of Revelation 11.

The timing of this power and authority coming to the saints coincides with the revealing of the ultimate evil of antichrist and the granting of his temporary power and authority. Notice how great darkness and great light are established and revealed on earth at the same time. The players are on stage for the great final battle between good and evil. The outcome of the entire war hinges on this final battle. God has created all things in preparation for the outcome of this battle which will demonstrate His wisdom through the Church to the devil and his angels.

Notice the unmistakable parallels between Jesus' time of public ministry and the walk of these saints. Both take place during a three and one-half year time frame. Both are initiated by the coming of the Holy Spirit in great power, anointing, authority; and both bring the Kingdom of God. Both take place amidst a time of intense Satanic government and religious persecution which ends in both parties physically overcome by Satan yet ultimately victorious. Both result in Satan's defeat.

It is crucial that we understand that Jesus died to overcome Satan, and yet He is authorizing and empowering His Church to also die to overcome Satan at the end of the age. (They overcame him by the Blood of the Lamb, the word of their testimony, and that they did not love their lives unto death.) Why is God allowing this seeming repetition? Didn't Jesus thoroughly overcome Satan on the cross two thousand years ago? Yes, He did. But the eternal plan of God in Christ Jesus is that through the **Church** God said He would demonstrate His wisdom to the rulers and authorities in the heavenly places.

God is going to use fallen mankind that Satan deceived to overcome Satan through the redemptive process enabled by His Son. That redemptive process is legally possible because Jesus came as a man, and as a man He legally overcame Satan on the cross. He specifically and purposely emptied Himself (Philippians 2:7) and came as a man to live and die as a perfect man in order to gain authority over Satan which He could then delegate to His Church, a corporate body of redeemed men.

The Church is called by faith to overcome Satan in the power and authority that Jesus has delegated. The death of the Church is obviously redemptive in God's plan, or the death of Jesus would have been the end of it. Scripture indicates that the primary purpose for Jesus' coming was to destroy the works of the devil (1 John 3:8). The Church does not yet realize that He accomplished that legally on the cross as a man in order to direct and authorize His Church to carry the sentence out on earth, ultimately by laying down their lives even as He laid down His life. This is the wisdom of the cross that God desires to demonstrate to Satan through redeemed man.

I have given You Power

God has seemingly chosen to use the Church, in the last three-and-one-half years of this age, to reflect the last three-and-one-half years of Christ's life and purpose for ministry on this earth. In fact, Jesus delegated everything that He came to do, short of the redemption of His Church, to His Church for accomplishment. He came to set the captives free, to heal the sick, to raise the dead, to reconcile Israel back to their God, to be a light of salvation to the Gentiles, to go into the world and make disciples of all nations, and to destroy the works of the devil. These are ongoing processes which have yet to be fully accomplished and have been delegated to the Church for completion. Ultimately it is Jesus Who does all these things, but all things short of the redemption of His Church are completed through the body of His Church. He gave us the power and authority to do these things and then said to go and do them in the power of His Spirit. **He came to enable us to do all the things that the Bible says He came to do.**

The specifics of the parallels between Jesus' time of public ministry and the ministry of the saints at the end of the age are intriguing and yet to be fully explored. These will surely be those days in which Jesus said His disciples would do even greater things than He did. I believe this is the Church on earth in its final and finest hour. This fully empowered and anointed Church will be the target of Satan's final and ultimate fury in the form of his champion, the antichrist. God has scheduled events so that His fully empowered Church and the evil of Satan in the form of the antichrist will appear on the earth at the exact same time.

God's power will be demonstrated through the meekness of His Church, for Scripture clearly indicates that Satan is granted power sufficient to physically overcome the Church.

God will demonstrate His wisdom by allowing this portion of the Church to be physically overcome, even as He allowed His Son to be physically overcome on the cross.

The wisdom of God in the form of the cross of Christ (1 Corinthians 1:24) demonstrated by Jesus as an individual will again be demonstrated at the end of this age by Jesus as His corporate body.

It is this staggering restatement of God's wisdom in Jesus Christ as demonstrated through His Church that will fulfill the Ephesians 3:10 intent **to demonstrate God's wisdom through the Church to the rulers and authorities in the heavenly places.** This is the glorious destiny the Church is called to. We have the privilege of walking as Jesus walked so as to have God's wisdom demonstrated through us.

That demonstration must incorporate all of Church history; however, the ultimate demonstration would seem to be the battle fought at the end of this age between the fully empowered Church and the darkest evil of antichrist. No wonder a great cloud of witnesses is watching and waiting for the Church to fulfill a destiny without which they cannot be made perfect (Hebrews 11:40-12:1). And no wonder Satan is so eager to keep the Church from fulfilling this destiny.

A calling awaits the Church at the end of this age which has all creation standing by until it is accomplished. It is something so staggering that prior saints cannot be made perfect without it.

We are called to run this race with endurance (Hebrews 12:1). We are called to fix our eyes on Jesus as an example during this race and to consider that He endured the cross for the joy set before Him so that we, in turn, do not grow weary and lose heart (Hebrews 12:2-3).

How vastly this scenario differs from teachings that assure us that we will be raptured away before the tribulation starts. Jesus will bring to completion His purposes **through His corporate body**. Therefore, it would be equally as illogical to say that the saints should be raptured out before the last three and one-half years of their ministry at the end of the age as to say that Jesus should have been raptured out before the last three and one-half years of His public ministry. God's purposes are that both parties should demonstrate the wisdom of the cross in seemingly the same manner.

The last-days persecution of the saints will not entirely be between believers and non-believers, but to a large extent, between those of a perverted religious structure and those who follow Jesus. Even as the religious leaders of Jesus' day persecuted Him and delivered Him up to be killed, so will a corrupt Babylonian religious system serve the saints up to be killed by a one-world government antichrist system.

Jesus foretold of a time when His disciples would be delivered up to be killed by those who would think they were doing God a service (John 16:2). Mystery Babylon is drunk with the blood of the saints and the witnesses of Jesus (Revelation 17:6).

Much of what we consider today as good is nothing more than religious structure. It is a man-conceived and upheld structure with a form of godliness but denying the power of the true gospel. If we are not walking with Jesus and being led moment by moment by His Spirit, then we are walking with and being led by another spirit, the spirit of the antichrist. I shudder to think where the dividing line may be in this confrontation. Jesus said family members would betray one another and brother would betray brother.

Are other Reasons for Jesus' Death Applicable to the Church?

Obviously the Church could not die to save itself. It would not have been an adequate sacrifice. There is only one perfect Lamb of God. But now that Jesus has gained the victory and delegated His power and authority to His Church, what other purposes which Jesus established by His death might also be parallel purposes for the death of His Church?

The purified and glorious Church during the last three and one-half years of the age will be Jesus' body. This won't be about us. It will be about Jesus living and dying through us. We can aspire to be nothing greater than cleansed vessels to be used for noble purposes. But to what noble purposes? To what extent might the death of that perfected body be considered redemptive in the restoration of the creation groaning for redemption? For example, to what extent might the death of that perfected body be considered redemptive in the restoration of Israel as a nation? What life will spring forth from the seed of the Church laying down her life? What multitude of sins might be covered by this love, a love which can prove no greater demonstration of its existence than by the laying down of earthly life? What redemptive purposes might God have awaiting this demonstration of love from potentially millions if not billions of His saints?

> This is My commandment, that you love one another, just as I have loved you. Greater love has no one than this, that one lay down his life for his friends (John 15:12-13).

The Return of a Favor?

In the previous chapter on redemptive suffering, we explored Scriptures that indicate that the nation of Israel has in part been turned over to disobedience in order that Gentiles could partake of the salvation offered through the Jews. How intriguing is the thought that even as Jesus died for the sins of His nation, so His corporate body, which will be largely Gentile, might fill up what is lacking in His suffering for the redemption of that nation.

> And now says the LORD, who formed Me from the womb to be His Servant, to bring Jacob back to Him, in order that Israel might be gathered to Him (For I am honored in the sight of the LORD, and My God is My strength) ... (Isaiah 49:5).

We have seen that the Church is called to die to overcome Satan even as Jesus died for the same purpose. We see also that Jesus came to die in order to restore Israel back to their God. If the reasons for Jesus coming to die apply as well to His Church, and I believe Scripture is clear that they do, then the death of the Church will also be redemptive in that restoration as she assists in filling up what is lacking in the sufferings of Christ (Colossians 1:24).

We are seeing staggering parallels between the life of Jesus and the walk of His Church at the end of the age, both in timing and function. As Jesus came to His nation but was rejected two thousand years ago, will He come again through His corporate body to again lay His life down? Will God again use the sufferings of His Son in the form of His Church as redemptive seed for the nation of Israel? When this happens, the eyes of Israel will be opened.

The Church as Suffering Servant

I believe that in this context the suffering of the Church is a possible third application for the suffering servant of Isaiah 53, who dies specifically for the sins of the nation of Israel.

I believe the willingness of the Church to lay down her life for the nation of Israel at the end of the age will perhaps be the demonstration of the cross through the corporate body of His Son that God is seeking before He turns again to His chosen people and pours out His mercy to restore that nation. Perhaps it will be this demonstration of love by their Christian brothers that will drive them at long last to jealousy. Perhaps it will be this that will prompt Israel to cry out, "Blessed is the One Who comes in the name of the Lord!"

The purposes for which Jesus came, which have yet to be fully worked out, will be fully worked out at the end of the age when His corporate body fills up what is yet lacking in His suffering. Satan **does not** want the Church to understand this. He wants her to be deceived, and if possible, fall away before her glorious destiny can be fulfilled, because his trip to the lake of fire is tied in with that destiny. Once again, I believe that much of his effort to deceive up to this point has been in the form of teachings which insist that the Church has no reason to be on earth during the upcoming period of great tribulation at the end of this age. It is the Church's demonstration of the wisdom of the cross during that great tribulation that is the very reason for which God created all things.

There is nothing of virtue that man has to offer in this process. We are at best empty and cleansed vessels through which Jesus can flow unhindered. This is not about anything the Church originates or brings to pass. This is about Jesus. When He gave up His life and said, "It is finished," He gained total victory over Satan.

Nevertheless, He has chosen to involve His Church in the victory over evil. It's His choice because He paid the price and gained the victory. Who are we to question His motives? We can only say, "Yes, Lord," to His plan. His plan happens to involve the Church, not of her own goodness, but of His goodness which He has chosen to demonstrate through her. Everything that the Church will demonstrate at the end of the age that is life-giving and of value will be of Jesus. He will relive and complete His purposes through His corporate body. We must individually decrease so that He can increase. We must die to ourselves so that He can live and die again through us.

> The Spirit Himself bears witness with our spirit that we are children of God, and if children, heirs also, heirs of God and fellow heirs with Christ, if indeed we suffer with Him in order that we may also be glorified with Him (Romans 8:16-17).

A Light of the Nations

> He says, "It is too small a thing that You should be My Servant to raise up the tribes of Jacob, and to restore the preserved ones of Israel; I will also make You a light of the nations so that My salvation may reach to the end of the earth" (Isaiah 49:6).

The vision of the suffering servant of Isaiah 53 grows to embrace all nations, tribes, tongues, and peoples.

> Arise, shine; for your light has come, and the glory of the LORD has risen upon you. For behold, darkness will cover the earth, and deep darkness the peoples; but the LORD will rise upon you, and His glory will appear upon you. And nations will come to your light, and kings to the brightness of your rising (Isaiah 60:1-3).

Technically this Scripture would seem to apply to Israel, but the Holy Spirit has quickened this in application to the Church as well at the end of the age. In the sequence of events, light will come first from the Church before it comes forth from Israel. It will be the light of Christ through His Church that will illuminate darkened Israel from their centuries of sleep.

> Awake, sleeper, and arise from the dead, and Christ will shine on you (Ephesians 5:14).

We must develop and embrace a theology that allows for the systematic slaughter of potentially several billion Christians at the end of the age, and we must understand that it is an outworking of God's love for the restoration of His creation. In light of eternity, it is a trivial price to pay, but it requires faith to see things in eternal perspective. That is a challenge that few if any theologians have met. I presently have difficulty embracing minor obstacles that the Lord puts in my path and call them God's love. The potential slaughter of several billion of our brothers and sisters, ourselves included, is the theology which we must rise to embrace.

We must learn to live only for Him now, or we shall not live for Him then. We must die to ourselves before that day, or we shall not be able to die for Him on that day. The journey is too great. Grace is our only hope. Without God's grace poured on us at the end of the age, we will never endure and rise to this call. Our best laid beliefs and doctrines will not support us at the chopping blocks. Only the grace of God will get us through. He must be our victory or we will have no victory.

Will it be Jesus or the Church?

The astonishing parallels between Jesus' time of public ministry and the walk of the Church during the last three and one-half years of the age make it hard to distinguish between who is Jesus and who is His Church. But Jesus **is** His Church! When we hesitate to ascribe this glorious walk to the Church because we feel it diminishes from what Jesus has already accomplished, we miss the point. This **will be** Jesus walking at the end of the age, but through His corporate body.

When pride and selfishness are totally burned out of us, we will not presume to see this as stealing His glory, but rather as glorifying Him. Of Him and through Him and to Him are all things. This will be the walk of a selfless devoted body of believers who seek nothing for themselves and everything for His glory. Only then and in that state will they be considered as worthy vessels for the power and authority that He intends to demonstrate through them. They will seek only to follow the Lamb wherever He goes, and as He walks so they will walk. He is calling us to lay down our lives for the same purposes that He laid down His life. Those who seek to follow the Lamb will be expectantly and joyfully prepared to do so.

We will Live the Vision

As we meditate on this biblical vision for the Church, it will turn our gaze toward Him, for surely the journey is too great for any of us. Without Him we can do nothing, but in Christ all things are possible. We will increasingly be conformed to the soldiers that Jesus would have us be at the end of the age. We will increasingly become like Jesus. We will set our faces like flint toward the destiny before us, seeing the eternal joy that awaits at the end of our endurance.

We will not be able to speak a message of hope and joy to a world writhing in the agony of birth pains unless we live that message, not just in the words that we speak but more importantly in the demonstration of our very lives.

Anything less is a false witness. If we do not portray Jesus by our lives, we betray Him by speaking of Him. We cannot be the good news if we are the bad news. The Kingdom of God is not a matter of words but of power.

If we cannot bring bread to the hungry and healing to the sick, we are not walking the walk that Jesus walked, and we are not allowing His life to flow through us to the degree that He insists upon. If we cannot portray to the lost masses the Bread of Life, then we are limiting Him. Our failure will not be that we are lifeless; it will be that we obstructed the flowing of His life through us. Perhaps we thought it was about something that we had to offer, when all along it was only of Him. We cannot of ourselves be loving. We cannot of ourselves be anything good, as He is everything that is good. It is only as we partake of Him and allow His life to flow through us that love or anything else of value can be demonstrated. Only what's done **by** Christ will last. The rest is but wood, hay, and stubble . . . the works of the flesh done on a foundation of sand.

Restoring the Stolen Vision

I believe we have now recovered a portion of the vision for the Church which has been stolen by Satan. The vision is clearly outlined in Scripture. The heart of God for His Church is to demonstrate His wisdom through His Church to the rulers and authorities in the heavenly places by overcoming the devil while conforming us to the likeness of Jesus. All of creation will be restored in the process. Everything that happens in our lives is a means to that end. The path that Jesus walked is the path for us to walk. It involves a choice and leads to the cross. The wisdom of God is the cross of Christ, and as we embrace the cross the vision will be realized. There are no shortcuts or alternate paths. The path is narrow and not without obstacle. Satan will scratch and claw and fight us every step of the way. It is a fight to the finish, a fight for survival, and even if we don't realize it, he does. He pulls no punches, fights dirty, and has a contract out on each of our lives. He wants us to fall away and not realize the vision and fulfill our calling. He does not want creation restored and God to be glorified, and he does not want to be crushed underfoot and thrown into the lake of fire. But he will be. Praise the Lord!!

The Final Act

This will be our last opportunity for worship this side of eternity. It will be the last opportunity to lay down our lives in obedience and love before we are swept up in the glory to come, beyond which we have no inkling of what God has prepared for us. The laying down of our lives may well be seed that sweeps many into the Kingdom with us. What more glorious destiny on this earth could there be? Embrace the cross, Saints, for the glory of our Lord and our eternal joy in His presence!

"This is all about You, Jesus. It's all about You."

EIGHT

Follow Me!

He said to him the third time, "Simon, son of John, do you love Me?" Peter was grieved because He said to him the third time, "Do you love Me?" And he said to Him, "Lord, You know all things; You know that I love You." Jesus said to him, "Tend My sheep. Truly, truly, I say to you, when you were younger, you used to gird yourself, and walk wherever you wished; but when you grow old, you will stretch out your hands, and someone else will gird you, and bring you where you do not wish to go." Now this He said, signifying by what kind of death he would glorify God. And when He had spoken this, He said to him, "Follow Me!" Peter, turning around, saw the disciple whom Jesus loved following them; the one who also had leaned back on His breast at the supper, and said, "Lord, who is the one who betrays You?" Peter therefore seeing him said to Jesus, "Lord, and what about this man?" Jesus said to him, "If I want him to remain until I come, what is that to you? You follow Me!" (John 21:17-22).

Peter was told by Jesus, at last, after all of his questions, **"What is that to you? You follow Me!"** Isn't that what we are all told? We have at best a dim sense of even our own individual destinies. Some of us will remain until He comes; some of us will go to Him sooner and glorify God with our physical deaths. In between now and then, the details are the Lord's details.

It is sufficient to know that we are to follow Jesus. He will lead us along the unique and perfect path that He chose for us before time began. And along that path He will never leave us or forsake us, even though there may be moments in lesser Gethsemanes and lesser Calvarys. There will be moments when the flesh is weak, even though the spirit wills. There will be moments of stumbling, but in order to purify and refine. But there will never be a moment when He leaves or forsakes us. Our trust of that even in the midst of discipline and the absence of all objective evidence of His presence is the measure of our trust in Him. It is **this** trust, it seems, that pleases Him most. It is the trust of Job sitting in the ashes. It is the trust of Abraham with the knife raised.

There will never be a moment during our lesser Calvary when we will need to cry out, "My God, My God, why hast Thou forsaken Me?" We will never have to die that kind of death, because He died that death for us. He died with the sins of the world on Him. We will not. He became sin for us. The deaths that we are called to will be like that of Stephen, when he looked into heaven and saw Jesus standing at the right hand of the Father. There was no sense of being forsaken when Stephen was martyred. It is questionable that he even felt the stones. And then he fell asleep. Such will be the grace of God for those of us who will glorify Him with our deaths. When we stand in front of governors and kings of the antichrist system, we are told to not worry about what we will say because it will be given us. There will never be a moment when what comes to us is not from, or by allowance of, His hand for our ultimate good. All things work to the good for those who love God and are called according to His purpose. There will consequently never be a moment unworthy of rejoicing in and trusting in and thanking and praising Him, Who has promised to bring to completion in each of us that good work which He began.

> Rejoice always; pray without ceasing; in everything give thanks; for this is God's will for you in Christ Jesus (1 Thessalonians 5:16-18).

Whether we are chosen to glorify God with our deaths or chosen to glorify Him by remaining until He comes, let us settle once and for all that we will follow Him. Where else will we go? He has the words of life.

> For I am convinced that neither death, nor life, nor angels, nor principalities, nor things present, nor things to come, nor powers, nor height, nor depth, nor any other created thing, shall be able to separate us from the love of God, which is in Christ Jesus our Lord (Romans 8:38-39).

To Follow Him, Keep Your Eyes on Him

It is so easy to take our eyes off what is essential and focus them on things of lesser importance. Our works and our ministries vie for our attention. The statement suggests the problem. It must not be *our* works and *our* ministries, but His. How often our business is not associated with His chosen works for us. The danger of focusing on anything other than our Savior is that we will find ourselves sinking beneath the waves.

That is the danger of the times ahead. Peter was doing fine until he took his eyes off Jesus and became concerned with the weather. We will do fine as we keep our attention focused on Jesus, whether we are in or out of the boat. There are many things in the days ahead that will scream for our attention, yet only one thing is important. Mary had it and so must we. Business in the kitchens of life is never as important as the thing which is primary, and that is to keep our focus on Jesus, listen to what He says, and do it. The only business in the kitchen we should be doing is that business He tells us to do. The clamor of the world's voices will always try to divert our attention from that voice which is primary. And it was Jesus that Martha was serving. It is the business of the *ministry* that will be the most subtle in diverting our eyes from that which is primary.

Peter had to learn that Jesus could be trusted, but Peter could not be. He had to be taken through painful experiences until he realized this. But it was the key to his freedom and the beginning of ministry in the power and authority of Jesus. He finally took his eyes off himself and focused on Jesus. He realized there was nothing good in Peter except Jesus Who lived in Him by faith.

Important but Secondary Issues

We have talked much about restoration of the vision of the Church and the call of the Church, but these are secondary issues. They are issues of doctrine and ministry. They are often issues of being busy in the kitchen. Giving up our lives will never be possible if we take our eyes off Jesus. Stephen gazed into heaven and saw Jesus standing at the right hand of God. Therefore, he could receive the stones. We must be gazing into heaven when our stones come. We must be gazing into heaven when the edict comes to take the mark of the beast or forfeit our lives and the lives of our families. We must have our eyes on Jesus or we will be seduced by the false security the world offers when our times of testing come. The many who will fall away and those whose love will grow cold will fail to endure because their eyes were not on Jesus.

> Hence, let us go out to Him outside the camp, bearing His reproach. For here we do not have a lasting city, but we are seeking the city which is to come (Hebrews 13:13-14).

The timing and nature of end-time events are secondary issues. They are important, however, in that they have the potential to cause us to stumble and take our eyes off Jesus. But that makes them very important. Therefore, it is necessary that we understand as much about them as God would have us understand. The study of these events must not be an end in itself, but a means of revealing stumbling blocks that could cause us to lose sight of the larger issue at hand. And that issue is that these events are birth pains preceding our births into the likeness of Jesus.

> These things I have spoken to you, that you may be kept from stumbling . . . But these things I have spoken to

you, that when their hour comes, you may remember that I told you of them (John 16:1,4).

Jesus is saying that the very reason we have been given these prophetic details of what lies ahead for the Church is so that we will **not** stumble when these things come. Otherwise we would have no need to know. There are many things we don't know. The voices of the seven thunders are concealed. But Jesus has told us what we need to know so that we will not stumble.

Stumbling Blocks at the End of the Age

> And he causes all, the small and the great, and the rich and the poor, and the free men and the slaves, to be given a mark on their right hand, or on their forehead, and he provides that no one should be able to buy or to sell, except the one who has the mark, either the name of the beast or the number of his name (Revelation 13:16-17).

> And another angel, a third one, followed them, saying with a loud voice, "If anyone worships the beast and his image, and receives a mark on his forehead or upon his hand, he also will drink of the wine of the wrath of God, which is mixed in full strength in the cup of His anger; and he will be tormented with fire and brimstone in the presence of the holy angels and in the presence of the Lamb. And the smoke of their torment goes up forever and ever; and they have no rest day and night, those who worship the beast and his image, and whoever receives the mark of his name." Here is the perseverance of the saints who keep the commandments of God and their faith in Jesus. And I heard a voice from heaven, saying, "Write, 'Blessed are the dead who die in the Lord from now on!'" "Yes," says the Spirit, "that they may rest from their labors, for their deeds follow with them" (Revelation 14:9-13).

A time is coming at the end of the age during the great tribulation when those who die in the Lord and rest from their labors will be considered blessed. These are times that Christians alive at the end of the age will experience. There is no option in dealing with the mark of the beast; the only correct choice is to refuse it.

Those who follow the course of monetary transactions and the trend toward a cashless society can see that the course is being charted by evil. The criminal element is dictating the precautions and safeguards and the inevitable march to a debit card that cannot be lost or stolen, even though it is all coming as an angel of light. National news magazines are forecasting a time when micro-chips presently being used on *smart cards* will be implanted under the skin. The mark of the beast is the inevitable destination for the course of monetary transaction. All universal product code markings on purchase items are now bordered left and right and divided in the middle by two narrow vertical lines which are the coded six. The number of the beast is already on almost all marketable products, including Christian books. Take a look at the next Christian book that you buy — maybe this book. On the back is coded a six-six-six in the universal product code. That is how subtle and unnoticed and yet pervasive this thing is. Automated check out lines at grocery stores using the bar code system are in the news. Ring it up and pay it automatically with your debit card. But what if someone steals your card? Hey, just implant the data chip under your skin. It makes perfect sense. It's going to be logical and convenient and safe . . . and eventually mandatory upon threat of death.

Refusal of the mark of the beast will mean the end of buying and selling for those without it. Without the mark, it will no longer be possible to go to a store and buy food and clothing. Public transportation, gasoline, medical care, utilities, and the basic essentials that we routinely purchase and take for granted may no longer be available. I'm looking forward to those days. Hey, let's get it on! Our Lord is coming back!

To refuse the mark will require the trust of the Hebrew children as they entered the fiery furnace and Daniel as he entered the lion's den. It will require the trust of Moses as he took the nation of Israel into the desert without food or water.

These need not and **must not** be times of anxiety. It is written that we are to cast all of our anxiety on Him. Our Heavenly Father is trustworthy. He has already demonstrated that He knows how to preserve a nation in the midst of a barren desert by raining manna from heaven and issuing water from a rock. He has demonstrated that the container of oil and of flour need not fail. He has demonstrated that He can shelter His people from plague and famine and wild beasts and fiery furnaces. These evidences of God's faithfulness are provided for the benefit of us upon whom the end of the age has come. He has never failed anyone who put their trust in Him.

If the Israelites had praised God in the desert instead of grumbling, their passage to the promised land would have been much quicker. If we should find ourselves three days in the desert without water, let's choose to praise God rather than grumble. Pray that we would all have the grace of strength to stand before Him and not deny Him.

Will I find Faith on Earth?

Many **will** fall away. These are not unbelievers, for unbelievers cannot fall away. These are believers who have fallen away from their trust, their faith, and their hope. The love of most **will** grow cold. Jesus questioned whether He would find faith on the earth when He returns. We have not concerned ourselves with what the end of this age is going to be like for those remaining on earth. We are going to have to live in the peace and rest of His presence when a thousand fall on one side of us and ten thousand fall on the other.

There are reasons why Scripture includes the passage that thousands will fall at our left and right but the plague will not touch us. The fourth seal and the sixth trumpet provide for the death of one-half of the earth's population during a time when the majority of the Church of Jesus

Christ alive at the end of the age will be living on earth (as opposed to having been raptured to heaven).

> Do not fear, for I have redeemed you; I have called you by name; you are Mine! When you pass **through** the waters, I will be with you; and **through** the rivers, they will not overflow you. When you walk **through** the fire, you will not be scorched, nor will the flame burn you. For I am the LORD your God, the Holy One of Israel, your Savior (Isaiah 43:1-3).

We are not promised escape from the midst of destruction, but we are promised protection through it. We must mature in our understanding of what God is going to do at the end of this age and how it relates to His Church. This can be the time of our greatest witness, or it can be the time of our love growing cold and of our falling away.

These are basic theological issues between the Creator and His created that have nothing to do with religion but have everything to do with relationship. It will be necessary that our holy fear of God be greater than our fear of man. The reality of His faithfulness must be greater to us than the reality of their guns and guillotines. Man can only kill the body but God can destroy both body and soul. These are times we will not survive without an ultimate abandonment to God that reserves nothing for self and its provision. The birthing described at the end of this age is the birthing of Jesus within those who have allowed the flesh and all things of self to be put to death in favor of His life.

A Brief Y2K Testimony

Being an engineer, my natural mind was whirring and ready to get well prepared for great tribulation or Y2K, whichever came first. I carried a can of Dinty Moore beef stew around in my van for almost ten years, and it didn't spoil, so I thought, "Ahaa! I have found the great tribulation staple." I began saving two-liter plastic soda bottles and was about to begin stockpiling rice, etc. But one morning while reading the reassuring promises in the Psalms, I felt led to ask the Lord if it would please Him if I did nothing. I immediately felt His presence and pleasure. So I did nothing. I didn't fill my tank up with gas. I purposely did not lift a finger or set aside one teaspoon of provision. And nothing happened as we all know.

I shared what I sensed the Lord was telling me with a few people, but I was never sure what to tell anyone else to do. I know the Lord told me to do nothing. But I couldn't say if that applied to anyone else. I couldn't say whether Y2K was going to be a non-problem or whether it was going to result in a global melt-down. I didn't know. But I know that He told me to do nothing. And I had peace and rest. When January First rolled around, I was as surprised as anyone that nothing happened. Okay, so what's the moral of the story?

The moral of the story is this. Who cares what's going to happen — Jesus is Lord! And if you seek Him, He will tell you what to do. Maybe for the great tribulation He will tell you to store food. Maybe He will tell you to do nothing. Do whatever He says! The greatest provision we have is Jesus! And He talks to us if we talk to Him! Who cares if the planet is going to melt down. Jesus is Lord! Read the Psalms. He says He's going to take care of us! Ask Him what He wants you to do and then do it in the full rest and peace of being in His will. Praise the Lord! Follow Him!

These are Times to Exercise Faith

These are the times to exercise faith for the days ahead. It is perhaps a time for discarding things rather than storing up. He alone is our gold and silver and our sustenance. Perhaps we should seek God about beginning to eliminate some of those things from our lives that we have always considered *essential.* If God is our protector, do we need life and health insurance? Do we need fire and theft and flood and hurricane insurance for our houses if angels are guarding the four corners of the property? Do we need our savings accounts, our retirement plans, our stocks and bonds, and our safety deposit boxes filled with gold coins? Do we need stored food? Saints, we had better not need them, for many of these things will be useless in the day of testing. If we cannot get along without these things now, will we be able to get along without them then? All of these things in which we presently put our trust will be of no use when the time of testing comes. For the time of testing is designed to remove all props which we count on for support. Only Jesus is worthy of our trust and support, and He alone must be our foundation in that day, for all other foundations will crumble. The more props we remove now, the easier it will be to stand in faith when all props are removed.

Anything that we consider essential or a support other than the faithfulness of God is an idol and will be stripped in the day of testing. Otherwise it would not really be a day of testing. The day of testing will reveal where we put our trust. That will be the point of the test. Ridding oneself of idols now will be easier than ridding oneself of idols then. It may even preclude the necessity of going through that time of testing. There is provision for avoiding the final crucible if the purifying fires of prior lesser crucibles have been embraced and allowed to do their work.

> Because you have kept the word of My perseverance, I also will keep you from the hour of testing, that hour which is about to come upon the whole world, to test those who dwell upon the earth (Revelation 3:10).

> Be on guard, that your hearts may not be weighted down with dissipation and drunkenness and the worries of life, and that day come on you suddenly like a trap; for it will come upon all those who dwell on the face of the earth. But keep on the alert at all times, praying in order that you may have strength [be accounted worthy, KJV] to escape all these things that are about to take place, and to stand before the Son of Man (Luke 21:34-36).

The better translation of *strength* is "to be accounted worthy." But whether it is strength or worthiness, it will be His strength and worthiness in us, vessels of clay trusting in the hand of the Heavenly Potter to do His perfect work in His perfect time. The absence of worries of life implies total trust. Those who are anxious and worried evidence unbelief which, if not burned away by the fires of purification, will preclude entry into the Holy City and result in burning by that other fire.

> But for the cowardly and unbelieving . . . their part will be in the lake that burns with fire . . . (Revelation 21:8).

Hoarding is Death

These must not be times of hoarding what little we might have left. It was only as the widow gave up her last oil and flour that it was multiplied and found sufficient until the days of famine were over. It was only as the lad gave up his few fish and loaves that they could be multiplied by Jesus to feed the multitudes.

We must give it all up before it will be multiplied. Whether we should be stocking our shelves or not, I do not know. But I do know that we must be prepared to give it all up when the needy knock at our door. It was the two small copper coins given by the widow at the temple that received the commendation of Jesus, for she had given it all, not just that which was surplus.

Hoarding is death. The lesson I have learned from hoarding is that the thing hoarded will never be adequate. It will spoil or be taken from the one hoarding so that **no** benefit will result from trying to hold onto it. **That which you try to keep you will lose.** It is a Kingdom principle. Secondly, the one with whom you would have shared it will not benefit from your provision, and you will have lost your reward. And thirdly, God will not be glorified in the process. This, for me, has been one of the hardest lessons to learn. I have not learned it well yet.

"Father, I confess my unbelief and my lack of trust in this area. I ask that You would cleanse me of this unrighteousness and give me the spirit of the poor widow who parted joyfully with her last copper coins."

Little children, guard yourselves from idols (1 John 5:21).

The Meek will Inherit

I have recently been attending meetings of those who have chosen to take an assertive stance in resisting the coming New World Order. Survival supplies, weaponry, self-sufficient communities, etc., are discussed. All of this is done in the assurance of being in the will of the Lord. I question whether the spirit of this is in the meek spirit of Jesus. It seems more often to be the assertive and self-reliant spirit of man. Are these the meek that will inherit the earth? Dare we take on the spirit of the lion while we are still called to walk in the spirit of the Lamb? How literal must we take the proverb to lean not on our own understanding? How literal must we take the following Scriptures?

> If anyone is destined for captivity, to captivity he goes; if anyone kills with the sword, with the sword he must be killed. Here is the perseverance and the faith of the saints (Revelation 13:10).

> Jesus therefore said to Peter, "Put the sword into the sheath; the cup which the Father has given Me, shall I not drink it?" (John 18:11).

When they came to arrest Jesus, Jesus restored the ear that Peter impulsively cut off. I have heard saints state in public teaching that if someone came to their front door and threatened their family, they would defend their family with an assault rifle. Is that what Jesus would do? We've got to respond in the Spirit at those times rather than in the flesh.

> For though we walk in the flesh, we do not war according to the flesh, for the weapons of our warfare are not of the flesh, but divinely powerful for the destruction of fortresses (2 Corinthians 10:3-4).

> So make up your minds **not to prepare beforehand** to defend yourselves; for I will give you utterance and

wisdom which none of your opponents will be able to resist or refute. But you will be delivered up even by parents and brothers and relatives and friends, and they will put some of you to death, and you will be hated by all on account of My name. Yet not a hair of your head will perish. By your endurance you will gain your lives (Luke 21:14-19).

"So make up your minds **not** to prepare beforehand to defend yourselves." This is in the context of verbal defense, but might it be general in application? No one could touch Jesus until it was His time. It wasn't that He was a master of self-defense; it was that His Heavenly Father was His defense. So it will be with each of us. If we try to influence that time in our own strength, we will have missed the point of total trust in our Heavenly Father Who only brings to our doorsteps what ultimately is good for us. I'm not preaching against assault rifles and storing up food, for I don't know what the Holy Spirit may tell you to do. I am preaching against doing anything without the leading of the Holy Spirit. May these words be a trumpet in your spirit that causes you to seek Him more aggressively, not necessarily to plan to defend yourselves more aggressively. I will not presume to know what He may tell you to do. Jesus demonstrated activism in the temple by turning over the tables and pacifism in Gethsemane by going meekly. If we are not listening obediently to the Holy Spirit, we will confuse the times. We must not rely on what we think or feel. **Total abandonment and trust and obedience to the Holy Spirit is the only right course of action in all situations.** There is coming a time when many of us will be asked to lay down our lives in the Spirit of the Lamb. If we respond in the wrong spirit, we will have missed the calling of God.

There will be a time for vengeance, but that vengeance is God's. When Jesus returns as the Lion of Judah, the winepress of God's wrath will be trampled. Until that time, we are counseled to walk this earth as lambs . . . wise as serpents, but gentle as doves. That counsel has never been revoked. It is no longer an eye for an eye. We are in a new covenant defined by the beatitudes. It is the wisdom of the cross that will overcome Satan, not our militancy.

Daniel in Babylon . . . an End-times Message to the Church

There was no better testimony in Babylon to the glory of God than that of Daniel and his three friends. We are also called to be a testimony in Babylon at the end of the age. Jesus says to us, "Come out of her, My people." I suggest that no one ever came more out of Babylon than did Daniel and his three friends, even though they lived most of their lives in her midst. Our physical location does not determine whether or not we have "come out of Babylon." Our unswerving devotion to our God and His Kingdom principles and the integrity with which we live our daily lives will determine whether or not we have come out of Babylon. These things will also determine whether our testimony in the midst of Babylon is of any value.

Jesus did not raise His voice in the streets or picket Rome and Caesar. His weapons were not carnal. He let His light shine forth in the midst of Caesar's Rome which released the power of the Holy Spirit to change lives from the inside out. Morality cannot be legislated. We should know that by now. Men's ways will not gain the victory. Jesus changed people by the wisdom of the cross. And when the knock on our door comes and we are told to worship our golden statue in the form of the image of the beast, we must refuse just like Daniel and his friends refused. There is a line not to cross. And we will trust God to rescue us from the fiery furnace or the lion's den or to allow us to lay down our lives for His redemptive purposes. It shouldn't matter to us one way or the other. Surrender to Babylon and live. Or let them kill you because they see the testimony of Jesus in you, not because you met them at the door with a sword, or bombed their headquarters, or holed up in the mountains in defiance.

The two witnesses who walk this earth representing the Church in peak power and authority during the last three and one-half years of this age do not respond to their enemies with rifle fire but with holy fire from out of their mouths. Did Peter do any differently when Ananias and Sapphira dropped dead? Our strength will not be found in our arsenals but in God's authority and power. There are no details on how the two witnesses die other than they are *overcome* at the end of their ministry. Their time had come to glorify the Father by their deaths. It was their cup to drink. It may have initially been bitter, but three and one-half days later it became very sweet. May it be the same for us at the end of our times of ministry.

"May we so glorify You, Father, with our lives and with our deaths."

PART TWO

Timing and Sequence of Key Events

NINE

The Timing and Sequence of Key Events

To the Church about the Church

The book of Revelation is written to the Church, for the Church, and about the Church. Most of the book deals with the key role the Church will play during the last three and one-half years of the age in God's eternal plan to demonstrate His wisdom through her to the rulers and authorities in the heavenly places. Identifying key players and properly ordering the timing and sequence of events is crucial to understanding the role and destiny of a Church brought to full power and authority to walk as Jesus walked in corporate world-wide demonstration of the true gospel.

Confusing key players and events blurs understanding of this role and destiny. Once again, Satan's clear intent is to confuse the Church about her role on earth during this period of time by convincing her that she won't be around, having no reason and purpose to remain on earth.

It is important to understand that Scripture says that not until the final three and one-half years of the age will the true gospel be preached world-wide. That is not to say that previous efforts have been fruitless, because it is obvious the Holy Spirit is working today and has been working throughout the age to convert sinners. There has always been a remnant on earth who have walked in the footsteps of Jesus. The work of the Holy Spirit today seems to be expanding exponentially world-wide. Perhaps we are very near to or even in the initial outflow of the prophesied great outpouring of the Spirit that will usher in the last and greatest harvest of the age. However, the true gospel of the Kingdom, not in words but in power, is not yet being preached world-wide the way Peter and Paul preached it. The Church will be largely unable to preach the gospel in this fullness of power before that time, because Scripture indicates that the Spirit will not be poured out in fullness until that time. This degree of power and authority does not come until the midpoint of the final seven years, concurrently with Satan being thrown out of heaven to earth. It is this outpouring of the Spirit that launches the ministry of the two witnesses and empowers the saints left on earth to overcome Satan by the Blood of the Lamb, the word of their testimony, and by loving not their lives unto death.

We think of effectively preaching the gospel in terms of stadiums filled with thousands. At the end of the age, however, when Christians will be persecuted and hated as criminals, spreading the gospel in any such manner will be forbidden. The account of the end of the age in the gospel of Mark implies that it will be as we stand under arrest before governing officials that the message of the gospel will go forth to the whole world. Our response during these times of persecution will be our witness of the true gospel. God will empower His saints to live sanctified, peaceful, and abandoned lives in the midst of furious persecution. This will be of greater witness to the unsaved than our words. The gospel will be demonstrated by how we live and die more than by what we say. The witness of today is often feeble, because we do not live what we say. Our lives are often a direct contradiction of the power of the gospel. Perhaps that is partly due to the lack of persecution which has always seemed to be the nutrient that causes the Church to flourish. But those times are changing.

More space is devoted to the last three and one-half years of the Church age in the book of Revelation than to all other periods of Church history combined. This period of time reveals the calling and destiny of the Church and identifies the standards of a Church brought to maturity in Jesus Christ. It defines the finish line of the race we are called to run. It establishes the vision without which we will perish. God has seemingly concentrated much of His plan to demonstrate His wisdom through the Church to the rulers and authorities in the heavenly places into the last three and one-half years of this age. During this short period of time, the ultimate destiny of the Church on earth, and the reasons for which she was created, will be fulfilled and demonstrated.

That is not to say that we can sleep until the start of the final three and one-half years. These are, at the very least, days of preparation. The time lines of these events seem somewhat blurred, as if the initial stages of judgment and glory are already at hand. The oceans and freshwater are already on the way to being polluted and unable to support life in many areas as if the judgment trumpets affecting these waters can be heard tuning up in the background. The prophesied great outpouring of the Holy Spirit at the midpoint of the final seven years seems to be gushing forth from cracks in the dam presently holding it back. The messengers of the end of the age are upon us. Regardless of the literalness or blurring of these time lines, the final three and one-half years of the age, as described in the book of Revelation, are the focal point of the vision of the Church at the end of the age. Regardless of the absolute timing of these events, these events establish the nature of that with which we must be concerned. I believe these time lines are absolute in the sense of the fullness of these prophesied events; however, I believe God in His mercy is also allowing a buildup of the preliminaries and initial stages of these events so that people wake up and repent. His judgments, ultimately, are redemptive. It is His will that none should perish.

The timing and sequence of events relative to the Church during this final three and one-half years of the age are the subject of our investigation. Teachings which remove the Church from the prophetic Scriptures involving the last three and one-half years of the age destroy all vision of the race we are called to run and finish. We have seen that God created all things in order to demonstrate His wisdom through the Church to the rulers and authorities in the heavenly places, and this demonstration will be largely fulfilled during the last three and one-half years of the age.

Removing the Church from this most crucial period of her destiny is to render null and void the eternal plan of God for His Church through which He will be glorified by all creation for eternity. Removing the Church from these times is one of the most grievous doctrinal errors that could ever be taught, and plays directly into the hands of the enemy of our souls. **The vision of the Church must be restored!**

"Father, would You release revelation in this area. Would You wake us up and give us a vision of eternal things and of the destiny of Your Church at the end of the age through which You will demonstrate Your wisdom and be glorified for eternity. Would You give us a passionate love for Your glory such that we might become noble vessels through which You can demonstrate Your wisdom and glory to the rulers and authorities in the heavenly places at the end of this age. Father, we pray to derail every effort of Satan to keep Your Church deceived about these things."

Benchmarks

I worked for the Forest Service one summer in Oregon doing survey work for logging roads. At the beginning, and periodically along every survey route (usually miles in length), we would establish *benchmarks* which were solid reference points (usually big nails driven into exposed roots or stumps). We could never make too big an error if we routinely referenced short sections of the surveyed route back to the benchmarks. These were the foundation reference points for the entire survey and kept us from losing a lot of time should an error creep into our work.

After we established our first benchmark at the start of the survey, we would then measure and sight out with a long tape measure and a survey scope to a distant survey point along the route, which would have been previously laid out with survey ribbons. When that point was established, we would record it and sight and measure out to a second point. After so many points, we would establish a second benchmark. Then we would sight back to the first benchmark and check to see that the loop would close. Then we would go on from the second benchmark to a third and so on until the route was completed. Perhaps it was symbolic that this was being done in the wilderness. The route had been walked out before and marked with orange ribbons where it should generally go, but we had to work out the details.

My own attempts to understand the prophetic Scriptures have proceeded in much the same way. Initially a few things seemed obvious, and I established these things as benchmarks and started from there. I thought that this might be one way to approach a study of the destiny of the Church during the last three and one-half years of the age. These are some of the benchmarks and survey points that I hacked out along my way. I hope this will be helpful to you. It is not in any way intended to be a comprehensive study of end-time events, but it does represent the foundation points that I believe the Lord has revealed in my own study relative to this message of restoring the vision of the Church. It would be helpful if the reader were already familiar with such concepts as Daniel's Seventy Weeks, the parallel of Jesus' warnings in Matthew 24 to the seven seals of Revelation, and had already struggled to understand the book of Revelation. I don't have space to fully develop the background for all of these areas. Any good prophecy book will discuss these things. Although most of the material on the shelves is pre-tribulation in nature, it is still useful to gain a background for what is discussed here.

Benchmark #1: The Great Tribulation is Over by the Sixth Seal

> For then there will be a great tribulation, such as has not occurred since the beginning of the world until now, nor ever shall. And unless those days had been cut short, no life would have been saved; but for the sake of the elect those days shall be cut short (Matthew 24:21-22).

> But immediately **after** the tribulation [the great tribulation of Matthew 24:21] of those days the sun will be darkened, and the moon will not give its light, and the stars will fall from the sky, and the powers of the heavens will be shaken . . . (Matthew 24:29).

These events involving the sun, moon, and stars match exactly the events of the sixth seal as described in Revelation 6:12-14. This can only mean that the seals prior to the sixth seal have been, in part, describing that great tribulation. This conclusion is supported in that the great multitude who show up in heaven in Revelation 7:14 **after** the sixth seal is opened, but **before** the opening of the seventh seal, are said to **have come out of the great tribulation.** The great tribulation would seem to be cut short by the startling events of the sixth seal.

This is a very important benchmark, because it establishes the entire framework of the timing of events of the book of Revelation. Jesus defined the great tribulation as that tribulation taking place after the abomination of desolation is revealed (Matthew 24:15). From Daniel 9:27 and 11:31, we understand that the abomination of desolation is revealed at the midpoint of the final seven years of the age, or three and one-half years before the end of the age. So by the sixth seal, conditions are already well into the last half of the final seven years of the age, because by the sixth seal, according to the words of Jesus, the great tribulation at the hands of antichrist is over.

Point 1: The spin-off from this is that most probably the breaking of the fourth seal and the persecution which results is revealing the reign of the antichrist and his false prophet, which begins at the midpoint of the final seven years. The fifth seal martyrs are then a direct result of that persecution.

Benchmark #2: The Trumpets Occur Late in the Last Three and One-Half Years of the Age

If the sixth seal takes place well into the last three and one-half years of the age, this automatically places the trumpet judgments (which follow the seals) even later in the last three and one-half years of the age. The plain wording of Scripture indicates that the trumpet judgments follow the seals. Perhaps the best indication of this is that the martyrs at the fifth seal are told to wait a little longer before God's judging and avenging begins. God's judging and avenging have, therefore, not yet begun at the fifth seal. The martyrs of the antichrist persecution are crying out to God from under the altar, "When will You avenge our blood?" The makeup of the sixth and seventh seals indicate that the beginning of the judging and avenging of God is in the form of the trumpet judgments and does not begin until the first trumpet is sounded.

Point 1: Since the sixth trumpet defines the end of the witness period of 1260 days of the two witnesses of Chapter 11, it follows that this 1260-day witness period of the two witnesses takes place during the last three and one-half years of the age. That is supported by the fact that their period of witness ends just before the blowing of the seventh trumpet, which by its very nature suggests the end of the age. It is reasonable to conclude, therefore, that the 1260-day witness period of the two witnesses coincides with the last three and one-half years of the age.

Point 2: The seventh trumpet, which sounds at, or very near, the end of the last three and one-half years of the age, is almost assuredly the last trump that Paul refers to in 1 Corinthians 15:52 as the trumpet sounding the harvest (rapture). This can be concluded because the harvest described at the end of Revelation Chapter 14 follows the three and one-half years of warfare between the antichrist and the saints. The events following the blowing of the seventh trumpet describe the rewarding of the saints and the destruction of the ungodly. These events match the makeup of the events of the Day of the Lord which are consistent with other passages describing the harvesting or gathering of the saints.

Benchmark #3: The Little Book of Daniel is the Little Book of Revelation

As mentioned previously, during a particularly strong visitation of the Holy Spirit one evening, I received a distinct impression that the little book of Daniel Chapter 12 was the same little book opened by the angel in Revelation Chapter 10. We must test all things with Scripture, however, and discard anything which does not match. In this case, Scripture matches with the impression, as the content of the little book of Daniel, which deals specifically with the last three and one-half years of the age, matches the content of Scripture immediately following in Revelation Chapter 10, which also deals with the last three and one-half years of the age. This would support the three and one-half year witness period of the two witnesses as being the last three and one-half years of the age.

Benchmark #4: Everything after Revelation Chapter 10 Deals with the Last Three and One-Half Years of the Age and Beyond

Much of what is presented in the later chapters of the book of Revelation is actually a *zoom-in* description in greater detail of what has been briefly covered in the earlier chapters. As we have seen, the great multitude of Chapter 7 are said to have come out of the great tribulation, so the events of the great tribulation must be associated with some of the five seals prior to the sixth seal. However, Chapters 13 and 14 describe in much greater detail the events of the great tribulation. Much of the book, therefore, has to be flashback and overlay. Understanding the book of Revelation becomes very confusing if the sequence of events is assumed to be laid out in a single series even as the chapters are laid out. The age has already come essentially to a close by Revelation 10:7.

> . . . but in the days of the voice of the seventh angel, when he is about to sound, then the mystery of God is finished, as He preached to His servants the prophets (Revelation 10:7).

Things seem to progress sequentially through the seals and trumpets up until the end of the age in Chapter 10. Then everything stops and the last three and one-half years are explored over and over again in more detail from different viewpoints as the details of the little book of Daniel are presented. The layout of Jesus' Olivet Discourse in the gospels is the same way. Jesus lays out sequentially the course of events up to the very end of the age at Matthew 24:14, and then stops and goes back over the last three and one-half years in more detail. When the angels tell John in Revelation 10:11 that he is to prophesy **again** concerning many peoples and nations and tongues and kings, that is indication of the start of the flashback. What follows is the last three and one-half years being described again and again from different perspectives.

Benchmark #5: Chapters 11, 12, 13, and 14 Repeatedly Cover the Last Three and One-Half Years of the Age

The witness period of the two witnesses of Chapter 11 is concluded to be the last three and one-half years of the age, as it ends just before the sounding of the seventh trumpet. The three and one-half year period the woman of Revelation 12 spends in the wilderness is then also concluded to be the last three and one-half years of the age. It begins with attempted persecution by the antichrist as he is revealed at the midpoint of the final seven years. The three and one-half year period of persecution of the saints of Chapters 13-14 is also concluded to be the last three and one-half years of the age. It also begins with the revealing of the antichrist and ends at the seventh trumpet just before the bowls of wrath are poured out. All periods of time identified in the book of Revelation as 1260 days, 42 months, or three and one-half years, are identified as the same period of time and as the last three and one-half years of the age. They are all revelations from the little book of Daniel 12, which deals specifically with the last three and one-half years of the age.

- Chapter 11:1-14 deals with the 1260-day witness period of the two witnesses. It is the first vision given after the little book of Daniel is opened.

- Chapter 12:1-14 deals with the simultaneous venture of the woman into the wilderness for three and one-half years.

- Chapter 13:1-18 deals with the antichrist and the simultaneous forty-two months of authority he is given over the saints.

- Chapter 14 deals simultaneously with at least a portion of the last three and one-half years from the time at which the 144,000 first fruits are seen in heaven until the harvest at the end of the age.

Benchmark #6: Revelation Chapter 14 Contains the Trumpet Judgments

Close inspection of Revelation 14 reveals that six trumpet judgments are described and are listed as taking place before the harvest at Revelation 14:14.

> And I saw another angel flying in midheaven, having an eternal gospel to preach to those who live on the earth, and to every nation and tribe and tongue and people; and he said with a loud voice; "Fear God, and give Him glory, **because the hour of His judgment has come;** and worship Him who made the **heaven and the earth and sea and springs of waters"** (Revelation 14:6-7).

The heaven, the earth, the sea, and the springs of water are the subject of the first four trumpet judgments, though not in that exact order. Since these four things are mentioned in conjunction with the coming of God's hour of judgment, the logical conclusion is that these are indeed the first four trumpet judgments. The fifth trumpet judgment is torment of those who do not have the seal of God on their foreheads, and it correlates with the torment of those who accept the mark of the beast in Revelation 14:9-11. The sixth trumpet judgment of the two hundred million man army from the east matches Revelation 14:8 which is the destruction of Babylon the Great described also in Revelation 17:16-18 and the whole of Revelation 18. Two hundred million soldiers marching from the east resulting in the death of one-third of the earth's population involves issues larger than the relatively small population of Israel. The economic and power structure of the entire planet is in turmoil. Although the order is shuffled, the identification of six distinct judgments identified with the coming of God's hour of judgment — which just happen to match the makeup of the first six trumpet judgments — cannot be just coincidence. These must indeed be the trumpet judgments. This conclusion is supported by the outpouring of the bowls which immediately follows in Chapter 15.

Point 1: And yet, amidst these apparent trumpet judgments and after the great tribulation has ended, there are saints who remain and are called to persevere unto death.

> Here is the perseverance of the saints who keep the commandments of God and their faith in Jesus. And I heard a voice from heaven, saying, "Write, 'Blessed are the dead who die in the Lord from now on!'" "Yes," says the Spirit, "that they may rest from their labors, for their deeds follow with them" (Revelation 14:12-13).

Point 2: The great multitude from **all** tribes, tongues, nations and peoples of Revelation Chapter 7 **cannot** have shown up in heaven before Revelation 14:6, because they must have already had the gospel preached to them (and this must have been world-wide) in order to be saved. But they must have shown up by the start of the trumpet judgments of Revelation 14:7. So the sixth seal logically must fall between

Revelation 14:6 and 14:7. The 144,000 first fruits who show up in heaven at Revelation 14:1 must have then arrived there sometime before the opening of the sixth seal.

Point 3: By the time of the harvest of Revelation 14:15, six trumpet judgments have taken place. The harvest is consistent with the events that take place at the blowing of the seventh trumpet. What remains of God's judging and avenging are the bowl judgments, which immediately follow. Those who show up in heaven before the harvest at Revelation 14:15 are either first fruits, or martyrs, or those who have died by natural causes.

Benchmark #7: The Great Multitude at the Sixth Seal are Martyrs, not Raptured Saints!

This is a major point of concern, as many believe that the great multitude at the sixth seal is the raptured Church. There is danger in teaching the timing of the rapture too early in the sequence of end-time events. If the great multitude are martyrs rather than raptured saints, then those who find themselves not raptured before the beginning of the trumpet judgments may be shaken to learn that they must continue to endure. I believe there is sufficient Scriptural evidence to conclude that these sixth seal saints are martyred rather than raptured saints.

> And when He broke the fifth seal, I saw underneath the altar the souls of those who had been slain because of the word of God, and because of the testimony which they had maintained; and they cried out with a loud voice, saying, "How long, O Lord, holy and true, wilt Thou refrain from judging and avenging our blood on those who dwell on the earth?" And there was given to each of them a white robe; and they were told that they should rest for a little while longer, **until the number of their fellow servants and their brethren who were to be killed even as they had been, should be completed also** (Revelation 6:9-11).

Point 1: God's judging and avenging of the martyrs' blood has not yet begun at the fifth seal. This supports, as previously mentioned, the conclusion that the trumpets and seals do not overlap, for God's judging and avenging of their blood does not seem to begin any earlier than at the first trumpet judgment. The sixth seal is stated in Revelation 6:17 as the indicator of the beginning of the day of God's wrath, and that wrath only begins when the seventh seal is broken and the trumpet judgments begin.

Point 2: The fifth seal martyrs are told that between the time when they are being addressed and when God's judging and avenging would begin, more of their fellow believers are to be killed. The next group to show up in heaven before that judging and avenging begins would then logically be those additional who are to be killed. The great multitude that shows up in heaven before the seventh seal is broken and the trumpet judgments begin fits exactly that description.

Point 3: The verses stating that they shall hunger and thirst no more, and that neither the sun nor heat shall adversely affect them anymore, and that every tear shall be wiped from their eyes, suggests that they have endured these things in the great tribulation. It is a solemn note to understand that these things will be necessary in order to conform these saints, who perhaps will be many of us, to the worthiness required to enter the Kingdom of God. This may be the most applicable prophecy for the majority of the Church alive at the end of the age. We may be reading of ourselves in these very Scriptures.

> And one of the elders answered, saying to me, "These who are clothed in the white robes, who are they, and from where have they come?" And I said to him, "My lord, you know." And he said to me, **"These are the ones who come out of the great tribulation,** and they have washed their robes and made them white in the blood of the Lamb. For this reason, they are before the throne of God; and they serve Him day and night in His temple; and He who sits on the throne shall spread His tabernacle over them. They shall hunger no more, neither thirst anymore; neither shall the sun beat down on them, nor any heat; for the Lamb in the center of the throne shall be their shepherd, and shall guide them to springs of the water of life; and God shall wipe every tear from their eyes" (Revelation 7:13-17).

Point 4: Another reason why I do not believe these are raptured saints is that Scripture indicates that the main harvest does not take place until the time of the seventh trumpet. Once again we need to be reminded that Jesus said that those who endure to the end, that end being the harvest, will be saved. Since we have already concluded that the seals and trumpets are sequential, those who show up in heaven following the sixth seal and before the seventh seal cannot be the same as those harvested at the seventh trumpet. The plain sense of Scripture is that the trumpets are held in check until the 144,000 of the tribes of Israel are sealed and the great multitude that no one could count from the great tribulation appears in heaven. It is the killing of this required number of additional saints that brings on the time when God begins His judging and avenging of their blood by the trumpet judgments, the beginning of His wrath. The first-fruits group at Revelation 14:1 are only listed as 144,000, whereas the multitude of the sixth seal is a great multitude which no one can count. This multitude without number is not the first fruits nor is it the general harvest. Therefore the multitude is concluded to be Christian martyrs who are the fulfillment of the prophecy of Revelation 6:11. And these are apparently not the last of the Christian martyrs, for there are more to be killed between the time of the sixth seal and the seventh trumpet harvest.

> And I heard a voice from heaven, saying, "Write, 'Blessed are the dead who die in the Lord from now on!'" "Yes," says the Spirit, "that they may rest from their labors, for their deeds follow with them." And I looked, and behold, a white cloud, and sitting on the cloud was one like a son of man, having a golden crown on His head, and a sharp sickle in His hand. And another angel came out of the temple, crying out with a loud voice to Him who sat on the cloud, "Put in your sickle and reap, because the hour to reap has come, because the harvest of the earth is ripe" (Revelation 14:13-15).

> And the seventh angel sounded [the seventh trumpet]; and there arose loud voices in heaven, saying, "The kingdom of the world has become the kingdom of our Lord, and of His Christ; and He will reign forever and ever." And the twenty-four elders, who sit on their

thrones before God, fell on their faces and worshiped God, saying, "We give Thee thanks, O Lord God, the Almighty, who art and who wast, because Thou hast taken Thy great power and hast begun to reign. And the nations were enraged, and Thy wrath came, and the time came for the dead to be judged, and **the time to give their reward to Thy bond-servants the prophets and to the saints and to those who fear Thy name, the small and the great,** and to destroy those who destroy the earth" (Revelation 11:15-18).

We have seen that the 1260-day witness period of the two witnesses does not end until the events of the sixth trumpet are finished, and that this witness period matches the last three and one-half years of the age during which time the antichrist is given authority over the saints. The end of that period of time coincides with the blowing of the seventh trumpet. Those harvested at the end of Chapter 14 are seen immediately in heaven in Revelation 15:2 having emerged victoriously over the beast and the great tribulation. After this, the seven plagues are poured out. The content of the seventh and last trumpet matches with the events of the last trumpet that Paul refers to in conjunction with the rapture.

> In a moment, in the twinkling of an eye, at the **last trumpet;** for the trumpet will sound, and the dead will be raised imperishable, and we shall be changed (1 Corinthians 15:52).

This certainly sounds like the time of reward of the bondservants the prophets, the saints, and the small and the great. Some will argue that Paul couldn't know about the trumpets since the book of Revelation hadn't been written yet, but Paul didn't need to wait for this revelation until the book of Revelation was written. Paul received revelation directly from the Lord.

Benchmark #8: There are Two Phases of God's Wrath

> And I saw another sign in heaven, great and marvelous, seven angels who had seven plagues, **which**

are the last, because in them the wrath of God is finished (Revelation 15:1).

If the bowls are the finish of God's wrath, then the wrath of God must have started prior to the bowls. Phase 1 is the beginning of God's wrath in the form of the trumpet judgments. Many of God's elect will still be on earth during the trumpet judgments but will remain untouched by God's wrath, even as the Israelites were untouched by the plagues which went on around them in Egypt. This phase ends with the harvest at the seventh trumpet of Revelation 14:15. Phase 2 begins right after that with the pouring out of the bowls of wrath. There are still those remaining on earth who will repent and be saved during Phase 2, and they would correspond to the gleanings harvested at the sixth bowl.

Point 1: I believe Scripture suggests the trumpet judgments may be centered in the Middle East in order to directly influence Israel. Scripture says judgment is first to the Jew, then to the Gentile. The one-third of the earth affected by the seven trumpet judgments seems chosen so as to impact Israel most directly. The sixth trumpet judgment appears to be an army from the east marching towards Jerusalem. This would explain why the 144,000 bondservants from the tribes of Israel are sealed just before the start of the trumpet judgments so as to pass through them unharmed.

Benchmark #9: Seven Seals, Seven Trumpets, Seven Years

There is indication that the events of the seven seals detail the last seven years of the age. I was walking one day asking the Lord about the timing of these things, and I heard these words come out of my mouth, "seven seals, seven trumpets, seven years . . ." Once again, that would not constitute reason for establishing doctrine, but it seems to correlate with Scripture.

> And **he will make a firm covenant with the many for one week,** [one week of years or seven years] but in the

middle of the week he will put a stop to sacrifice and grain offering; and on the wing of abominations will come one who makes desolate, even until a complete destruction, one that is decreed, is poured out on the one who makes desolate (Daniel 9:27).

If this is the antichrist, then he will appear as a covenant maker at the beginning of the final seven years, and this matches the makeup of the first seal. A rider shows up on a white horse, but it definitely isn't Jesus. This isn't **THE RIDER** on the white horse of Revelation 19. This is an impostor. He is a peacemaker, but He is not the Prince of Peace; therefore his peace will be a temporary and false peace. The confusion often associated with identifying the rider on the white horse of the first seal is representative of the actual confusion that will result when he is revealed in the flesh. Many will mistakenly think he is the Christ. He will come as an angel of light. The first warning Jesus gave to His disciples in Matthew 24 was to beware of false Christs. The additional warnings He gave line up with the seals in the book of Revelation, and it is very likely, therefore, that His first warning lines up with the first seal. The rider of the first seal is revealed for what he really is at the three and one-half year point, and this would agree closely with the revealing of Death and Hades at the fourth seal if the seals were laid out year for year. If the seven seals represent seven years, then the seventh seal would be the last of the seven years, a year of God's increasing trumpet judgments upon the earth. The fifth trumpet is five months in length, so the trumpet judgments are boxed in to being more than five months but significantly less than three and one-half years in duration.

> For the LORD has a day of vengeance, a **year** of recompense for the cause of Zion (Isaiah 34:8).

Will the day of the Lord's vengeance, which seems to begin at the sixth seal and lasts through the seventh bowl, be one year in length?

Point 1: Many believe that Daniel 9:27 is referring to Jesus, and that He is the one making or confirming the covenant. This *split-week* approach holds that the first three and one-half years of the final seven years elapsed during

Jesus' time of public ministry, and the remaining three and one-half years take place at the end of this age. There is some logical basis for this if only Daniel 9:27 is considered. But there are other Scriptures that shed additional light on the matter of who the *he* of Daniel 9:27 is.

> And from the time that the regular sacrifice is abolished, and the abomination of desolation is set up, there will be 1290 days (Daniel 12:11).

If we back up from this verse in the text to Daniel 11:31, there we will find the description of the regular sacrifice being abolished and the abomination of desolation being set up. I drew a line and an arrow in my Bible at Daniel 11:31 noting that from this point on, there will be 1290 days. What is in view here is obviously the last three and one-half years of the age.

> And forces from **him** will arise, desecrate the sanctuary fortress, and do away with the regular sacrifice. And they will set up the abomination of desolation (Daniel 11:31).

The *him* who does this is **not** Jesus. You can clearly see that by reading about *him* and what *he* does in the verses immediately preceding Daniel 11:31. If this *him* is not Jesus but the antichrist, and this *him* sets up the abomination of desolation and stops the sacrifice three and one-half years before the end of the age, then who is logically the *he* of Daniel 9:27 who is described as doing the very same thing in the middle of the final seven years? Do Jesus and the antichrist both stop the sacrifice and set up the abomination of desolation at the midpoint of the final seven years? Does the midpoint of the final seven years occur twice, once two thousand years ago and again at the end of the age? I don't think that is a logical conclusion based on the information given in Scripture. Therefore I believe the final week of the seventy weeks of Daniel will be played out at the end of the age in one seven year chunk of time, the last seven years of the age.

Point 2: It is after the sixty-two weeks that the Messiah is cut off, not after sixty-two and one-half weeks, which would be the case if Jesus' public ministry were considered the first three and one-half years of the last week of Daniel's seventy weeks.

> Then after the sixty-two weeks the Messiah will be cut off and have nothing, and the people of the prince who is to come will destroy the city and the sanctuary. And its end will come with a flood; even to the end there will be war; desolations are determined (Daniel 9:26).

Point 3: I believe Scripture further indicates in Daniel Chapter 8 that the 70th week of Daniel is the final seven years of the age.

> Then I heard a holy one speaking, and another holy one said to that particular one who was speaking, "How long will the vision **about the regular sacrifice** apply, while the transgression causes horror, so as to allow both the holy place and the host to be trampled?" And he said to me, **"For 2300 evenings and mornings;** then the holy place will be properly restored." . . . "Son of man, understand that the vision pertains to the time of the end." . . . And he said, "Behold, I am going to let you know what will occur at the **final period of the indignation,** for it pertains to the appointed time of the end." . . . And in the latter period of their rule, when the transgressors have run their course, a king will arise insolent and skilled in intrigue. And his power will be mighty, but not by his own power, and he will destroy to an extraordinary degree and prosper and perform his will; he will destroy mighty men and the holy people . . . He will even oppose the Prince of princes, but he will be broken without human agency. And the **vision of the evenings and mornings which has been told is true;** but keep the vision secret, for it pertains to many days in the future (Daniel 8:13-14, 17, 19, 23-26).

This is clearly referring to the antichrist. And these 2300 days, which are 220 days short of seven years, discuss the abomination of desolation being set up in the holy place during the **final** period of the indignation. There is only one **final** period of the indignation, and that's the period of the indignation at the end of the age beginning at the midpoint of the final seven years of the age. The reason the vision is for 2300 days and not 1290 days is because it includes the **time of the regular sacrifice** as well as the time from when the abomination of desolation is set up until the holy place is restored. I believe this could be indicating that restored temple sacrifices may start 220 days after the beginning of the final seven years of the age. *Evenings and mornings* locks in the 2300 as days and not years, as it is an Old Testament term for the "evening and morning" sacrifices. If the antichrist comes as a peacemaker and a covenant maker seven years before the end, it is logical to consider that part of that covenant agreement might allow the long-awaited rebuilding of a new Jewish temple and the resumption of regular temple sacrifices.

Conclusions

We need to understand from these Scriptures that the main harvest, or the rapture, is presented consistently as coming very near the end of the last three and one-half years of the age — at the end of the age to which Jesus said we must endure. It would seem to come at the seventh trumpet just before the bowls of wrath are poured out. It appears that most of the Church is going to remain on earth during the trumpet judgments, because the seventh trumpet lines up with the end of the age and seems to describe the rewarding of the saints. This is still consistent with "not being appointed to wrath," because when God's wrath fell on Egypt, His chosen people were "not appointed to wrath." It went on around them but did not harm them. That was the point of the blood on the doorposts.

If it doesn't work out this way and the rapture comes sooner, that will be just fine. But we shouldn't count on it coming any sooner. If we settle in our hearts that it's going to come just before the pouring out of the bowls of wrath just like Revelation Chapters 14 and 15 suggest, we will be in the best state of mind to endure to the true end of the age. However, let's not get so caught up in the details of the timing and sequence of all of these events that we take our eyes off Jesus. Let's not let our doctrines become stumbling blocks if things don't work out the way we expected. Ultimately, Jesus said that He would come at an hour that we did not expect, so we are all going to be surprised one way or another when He comes.

If we keep our eyes on Jesus, keep the vision of the Church in mind, and keep filled to overflowing with the oil of the Holy Spirit, rapture timing will take care of itself, and no timing of event will cause us to stumble. Remember, the end of this age is going to be a time of our light shining forth in the midst of great darkness. We should expect to walk with great anointing through the midst of this, crushing Satan underfoot in the process. There are those spoken of in Daniel who will lead many to righteousness during these times and will shine like stars forever.

Let's get from this a freshening of hope, a strengthening of our faith and trust, and a fresh revelation of God's all-consuming love for His Church. I had a dream many years ago, even before I was saved, of Jesus returning in the sky. In my dream, I was longing for a change, because I was tired of the world as it was. What if it were all true and He was actually coming back? I looked up into the sky as if my eyes were being drawn to a spot . . . almost as if I was creating it in my dream because I wanted it so badly. All of a sudden, there He was, a small burst of light but getting bigger quickly. I can't express the emotion I felt even in the dream. It was like a floodgate broke open and everything was suddenly beautiful. My spirit surged in an explosion of joy! All troubles and wars and distress were forever done with and replaced with a feeling of total satisfaction and joy. I woke up.

Now **that** is worth waiting for! And it's really going to happen. I think it may have been a vision as well as a dream. I can remember the joy and expectation I used to have as a child during the Christmas holidays, childish though it may have been. That joy and expectation fizzled as the years and the world took over. But the **real** reason for that childish Christmas joy is nearly upon us! We will all be as joyous children on the day He returns. There is reason for our faith and hope and trust!

"Come quickly, Lord Jesus!" The Spirit and the Bride say, "Come!"

TEN

Logic Trains of Rapture Timing

Timing is Important... but Secondary

I initially accepted the pre-tribulation rapture teaching as a new believer because the popular Christian books on prophecy and end-times that I read at that time were all of that doctrine. And I must say that those books blessed and instructed me and helped me to grow in the Lord. In those times, the Lord spoke to me and taught me and revealed His unconditional love. Obviously the Holy Spirit was not totally grieved about this doctrinal matter and was developing more important foundational issues. It was only later, as I became more familiar with the Scriptures, that I became uneasy with the content of Matthew 24 and the parts of Daniel and Revelation that discuss the saints being warred against and overcome. I could not reconcile these passages with a pre-tribulation rapture, and there was something unsettling about how these passages were being so casually excused from being applicable to the Church.

As the years passed and the Lord seemed to be revealing a vision for the Church, a pre-tribulation rapture became more and more inconsistent with that vision. The primary issue for the Church at the end of the age is still not rapture timing, but how she will glorify God. However, as the end of the age draws nearer, the issue of timing takes on greater importance in the context of that primary consideration. God's plan for His Church dictates rapture timing, not vice versa. Any teaching that obscures the vision of the saints and is contrary to God's plan is a serious problem and will become more serious as the end of the age approaches.

Most popular end-times teaching deals with rapture timing as an end in itself rather than as a supporting role in God's plan to demonstrate His wisdom through the Church to the rulers and authorities in the heavenly places. When God's purpose and plan become foundational in the study of end-time events, the Church's presence on earth at the end of the age will be seen as mandatory. Any theology which removes the Church from the earth during the last seven years of the age fails to incorporate the primacy of God's reason for creating the Church, which is to overcome Satan in the power of Jesus Christ, thereby demonstrating His wisdom.

Paul said **not to be deceived in any way** regarding the timing of the day of the Lord. The timing of the day of the Lord, as we will see, dictates the timing of the rapture. If the Church misunderstands rapture timing, she will misunderstand her role on earth at the end of the age. Mistaken teachings about the timing of the rapture lead to mistaken understanding of God's plan for the Church. If we subscribe to teachings which obscure God's plan for His Church at the end of the age, we will have no vision and may be in danger of stumbling and even falling away as the events of the end of the age overtake us.

The thesis of this book is that the Church has a glorious destiny while on earth which will be only fully played out during the last three and one-half years of this age. In the following examples of Scriptures which deal with rapture timing, we will see that the Church is consistently and clearly portrayed as being on earth until the harvest at the end of the age.

Logic Trains of Rapture Timing

I want to present several different *logic trains*, as Scripture reveals, regarding the timing of the rapture. I call them *logic trains* because they are logical progressions of Scripture that follow tracks of thinking that end up at the same conclusion. They are composed of direct passages from Scripture which deal with the timing of the rapture. Although rapture timing is not the central issue of this book, it impacts the basic thesis because if the Church is not here during the last three and one-half years of this age, the thesis falls apart. Although the term *rapture* is not found in Scripture, the description of rising in the air to meet Jesus as described by Paul in 1 Thessalonians 4:17 is commonly called the rapture. Some will argue that such a thing as the rapture does not exist and is not taught in the Bible, but the Bible describes the dead and living being caught up in the air to meet Jesus. That's the event referred to interchangeably as the rapture, or the harvest, or the gathering of the saints in all that follows.

To repeat once again, it is Satan's intent to keep the Church unaware, unprepared, and deceived about her role on earth at the end of the age. He seems to know the Bible, and he must be aware of Romans 16:20 which says the Church will crush him underfoot. He must know that we win and he loses. But it will be a fight to the finish, and he will drag as many into the lake of fire with him as he can. He will not fight fair, and he will most often come as a deceiving angel of light. Please study these Scriptures carefully, asking the Holy Spirit to speak to you. Do not believe anything written in this book without the witness of the Holy Spirit. Ask Him to be your teacher and guide into all truth. The point of the following *logic trains* is that they all say the same thing. They all locate the timing of the rapture at the same general time, namely, at the harvest at a time known as the day of the Lord, late in or near the end of the last three and one-half years of the age.

Train #1: What did Jesus Say?

One short logic train can be composed of three sections (boxcars) of Scripture: Matthew 24:13, Matthew 13:39, and Revelation 14:14-16.

1. In Matthew 24:13, Jesus says, speaking to His disciples: **"But the one who endures to the end, he shall be saved."** Remember that He is answering the questions of His disciples in Matthew 24:3 regarding the end of the age, so that when He refers to the "end," He is referring to the end of the age.

2. Matthew 13:39 defines the harvest as the end of the age: **. . . and the harvest is the end of the age; and the reapers are angels.**

3. Revelation 14:14-16 describes that harvest. Notice that it comes at the end of three and one-half years (forty-two months) of persecution of the saints:

> And there was given to him [the beast] a mouth speaking arrogant words and blasphemies; and **authority to act for forty-two months was given to him.** And he opened his mouth in blasphemies against God, to blaspheme His name and His tabernacle, that is, those who dwell in heaven. And it was given to him to make war with the saints and to overcome them; and **authority over every tribe and people and tongue and nation was given to him.** And all who dwell on the earth will worship him, everyone whose name has not been written from the foundation of the world in the book of life of the Lamb who has been slain. If anyone has an ear, let him hear. If anyone is destined for captivity, to captivity he goes; if anyone kills with the sword, with the sword he must be killed. **Here is the perseverance and the faith of the saints** (Revelation 13:5-10).

> And another angel, a third one, followed them, saying with a loud voice, "If anyone worships the beast and his image, and receives a mark on his forehead or upon his hand, he also will drink of the wine of the wrath of God, which is mixed in full strength in the cup of His anger; and he will be tormented with fire and brimstone in the

presence of the holy angels and in the presence of the Lamb. And the smoke of their torment goes up forever and ever; and they have no rest day and night, those who worship the beast and his image, and whoever receives the mark of his name." Here is the perseverance of the saints who keep the commandments of God and their faith in Jesus. And I heard a voice from heaven, saying, "Write, 'Blessed are the dead who die in the Lord from now on!'" "Yes," says the Spirit, "that they may rest from their labors, for their deeds follow with them." And I looked, and behold, a white cloud, and sitting on the cloud was one like a son of man, having a golden crown on His head, and a sharp sickle in His hand. And another angel came out of the temple, crying out with a loud voice to Him who sat on the cloud, "Put in your sickle and reap, because the hour to reap has come, because **the harvest** of the earth is ripe." And He who sat on the cloud swung His sickle over the earth; and the earth was reaped (Revelation 14:9-16).

Jesus told His disciples that the one who endures to the end of the age will be the one who is saved. He also defined the end of the age as the harvest. These are His words, plain and simple, regarding His disciples' questions about the end of the age. That harvest, which He describes in Revelation 14:14-16, comes after a specific time period of three and one-half years during which the saints are given over to the antichrist to be warred against and overcome. During this time they are counseled to persevere, to keep the commandments of God, to keep their faith in Jesus, and specifically **NOT** to take the mark of the beast.

This is the primary teaching in the Bible on the timing of the rapture for the Church-at-large, because Jesus gave it to His disciples throughout the age without qualification. There is no higher authority in any Christian bookstore. These words of our Lord are directed to us. Do we have ears to hear?

Train #2: Therefore when YOU SEE the Abomination of Desolation

> Therefore when **you see** the abomination of desolation which was spoken of through Daniel the prophet, standing in the holy place (let the reader understand), then let those who are in Judea flee to the mountains (Matthew 24:15-16).

1. Jesus' disciples who would be alive at the end of the age are told in this passage that they will see the abomination of desolation. That suggests something about rapture timing. The abomination of desolation spoken of by Daniel is not revealed until three and one-half years before the end of the age. Jesus was therefore clearly indicating that the rapture does not come until sometime after this, because He said that His disciples alive at that time of the end would **see** the abomination of desolation. Jesus therefore places the timing of the rapture sometime during the last three and one-half years of the age. This is the same point that Paul stresses in his letters to the Thessalonians. The fact that those in Judea are specifically addressed does not mean that **only** those in Judea are addressed. As mentioned before, the disciples addressed here are His disciples throughout the age and are the same individuals who are told to go into the world and make disciples of all nations.

Train #3: 1 and 2 Thessalonians and the Day of the Lord

The content of Paul's two letters to the Thessalonians is specific regarding the timing of the gathering (rapture) of the saints. These Scriptures reveal that the rapture will occur at a time known as the day of the Lord. That day of the Lord will not come until the apostasy and the revealing of the man of lawlessness (the antichrist) have taken place. This again automatically places the rapture sometime in the last three and one-half years of the age, because Scripture is clear that the antichrist will not be revealed until the midpoint of the final *week* of Daniel at three and one-half years before the end of the age.

It is essential that we understand that Paul's letters to the Thessalonians establish two main points. First, that the gathering of the saints will occur at a time called *the day of the Lord*. Second, that this day of the Lord will occur sometime during the last three and one-half years of the age. These are among the clearest and most specific Scriptures in the Bible defining the timing of the rapture. I am saddened to read books that use these same Scriptures to support the pre-tribulation position, because these Scriptures are most clear in answering simply and plainly the *where and what* of the rapture question. They locate the rapture sometime during the last three and one-half years of the age on the day of the Lord.

1. 1 Thessalonians 1:10 and 1 Thessalonians 5:9 settle the fact that the Church is not destined for God's wrath. But 1 Thessalonians 1:6, 2:14, 3:3-4, and 2 Thessalonians 1:4-5 clearly state that we are destined for tribulation and affliction. If we are confused about the difference between tribulation and wrath, it follows that we will be confused as to the timing of the rapture.

> . . . and to wait for His Son from heaven, whom He raised from the dead, that is Jesus, **who delivers us from the wrath to come** (1 Thessalonians 1:10).

> **For God has not destined us for wrath,** but for obtaining salvation through our Lord Jesus Christ (1 Thessalonians 5:9).

> You also became imitators of us and of the Lord, having received the word **in much tribulation** with the joy of the Holy Spirit (1 Thessalonians 1:6).

> For you, brethren, became imitators of the churches of God in Christ Jesus that are in Judea, for you also endured the **same sufferings** at the hands of your own countrymen, even as they did from the Jews (1 Thessalonians 2:14).

... so that no man may be disturbed by these afflictions; for you yourselves know that we have been **destined** for this. For indeed when we were with you, we kept telling you in advance that **we were going to suffer affliction;** and so it came to pass, as you know (1 Thessalonians 3:3-4).

... therefore, we ourselves speak proudly of you among the churches of God for your perseverance and faith in the midst of all your persecutions and afflictions which you endure. This is a plain indication of God's righteous judgment **so that you may be considered worthy of the kingdom of God, for which indeed you are suffering.** For after all it is only just for God to repay with affliction those who afflict you, and to give relief to you who are afflicted and to us as well **when** the Lord Jesus shall be revealed from heaven with His mighty angels in flaming fire, dealing out retribution to those who do not know God and to those who do not obey the gospel of our Lord Jesus ... when He comes to be glorified in His saints **on that day** (2 Thessalonians 1:4-8, 10).

We are destined for tribulation but not for wrath. We will be delivered from tribulation and rescued from wrath on a day known as the day of the Lord.

But immediately after the tribulation of those days THE SUN WILL BE DARKENED, AND THE MOON WILL NOT GIVE ITS LIGHT, AND THE STARS WILL FALL from the sky, and the powers of the heavens will be shaken, and then the sign of the Son of Man will appear in the sky, and then all the tribes of the earth will mourn, and they will see the SON OF MAN COMING ON THE CLOUDS OF THE SKY with power and great glory. And He will send forth His angels with A GREAT TRUMPET and THEY WILL GATHER TOGETHER His elect from the four winds, from one end of the sky to the other ... Therefore be on the alert, for you do not know which day your Lord is coming. But be sure of this, that if the head of the house had known at what time of the night the thief was coming, he would have been on the alert and would not have allowed his house to be broken into. For this reason you be ready too; for the Son of Man is coming at an hour when you do not think He will (Matthew 24:29-31, 42-44).

> For this we say to you by the word of the Lord, that we who are alive, and remain until the coming of the Lord, shall not precede those who have fallen asleep. For the Lord Himself will descend from heaven with a shout, with the voice of the archangel, and with the trumpet of God; and the dead in Christ shall rise first. Then we who are alive and remain shall be caught up together with them in the clouds to meet the Lord in the air, and thus we shall always be with the Lord. Therefore comfort one another with these words. **Now as to the times and the epochs,** brethren, you have no need of anything to be written to you. For you yourselves know full well that the **day of the Lord** will come just like a thief in the night. While they are saying, "Peace and safety!" then destruction will come upon them suddenly like birth pangs upon a woman with child; and they shall not escape (1 Thessalonians 4:15-5:3).

2. Consider the context of the sentence, "Now as to the times and epochs, brethren, you have no need of anything to be written to you." The times and epochs of what? What has Paul just been talking about? He's been talking about the rapture! What he is referring back to regarding "times and epochs" is the rapture and can only be the rapture, otherwise the sentence structure makes no sense at all. And then he goes on to say, "For you yourselves know full well that the day of the Lord will come just like a thief in the night." This is a crucial point. He has just identified the "day of the Lord" as the time of the rapture. Paul confirms it in his second letter:

> Now we request you, brethren, with regard to the coming of our Lord Jesus Christ, and our **gathering together to Him,** that you may not be quickly shaken from your composure or be disturbed either by a spirit or a message or a letter as if from us, to the effect that the **day of the Lord** has come. Let no one in any way deceive you, for **it will not come unless the apostasy comes first, and the man of lawlessness is revealed,** the son of destruction, who opposes and exalts himself above every so-called god or object of worship, so that he takes his seat in the temple of God, displaying himself as being God. Do you not remember that while I was still with you, I was telling you these things (2 Thessalonians 2:1-5)?

Paul has just answered the question regarding the timing of the coming of the Lord Jesus Christ and our gathering together to Him (i.e., the rapture) by saying that the day of the Lord has not yet come, and that it will not come until the apostasy comes first and the man of lawlessness is revealed. He has placed the timing of the rapture sometime during the last three and one-half years of the age at a time known as the day of the Lord.

Unfortunately, expositors conclude anything they want from these Scriptures. They have been used to *prove* both pre and post-tribulation rapture timing. What does the Holy Spirit say in these Scriptures to you? Go over and over and over them again until you gain the witness of the truth as given by the Holy Spirit. We must set aside any preconceived doctrines and let the Holy Spirit reveal the intent of these Scriptures to us or we shall surely be deceived, for the enemy would have us be deceived if at all possible.

Train #4: 1 Corinthians and the Day of the Lord

> I thank my God always concerning you, for the grace of God which was given you in Christ Jesus, that in everything you were enriched in Him, in all speech and all knowledge, even as the testimony concerning Christ was confirmed in you, so that you are not lacking in any gift, awaiting eagerly the revelation of our Lord Jesus Christ, who shall also confirm you to **the end,** blameless in the **day of our Lord Jesus Christ** (1 Corinthians 1:4-8).

1. We are to eagerly await the revelation of our Lord Jesus Christ Who will confirm us blameless **to the end,** the **day of our Lord Jesus Christ.** Notice the consistency with the previous logic trains. The end is the harvest and is the day of the Lord.

Train #5: 2 Peter and the Day of the Lord

> But the present heavens and earth by His word are being reserved for fire, kept for the day of judgment and destruction of ungodly men. But do not let this one fact escape your notice, beloved, that with the Lord one day is as a thousand years, and a thousand years as one day. The Lord is not slow about His promise, as some count slowness, but is patient toward you, not wishing for any to perish but for all to come to repentance. But the **day of the Lord** will come like a thief, in which the heavens will pass away with a roar and the elements will be destroyed with intense heat, and the earth and its works will be burned up. Since all these things are to be destroyed in this way, what sort of people ought you to be in holy conduct and godliness, **looking for and hastening the coming of the day of God;** on account of which the heavens will be destroyed by burning, and the elements will melt with intense heat (2 Peter 3:7-12)!

1. Notice the consistency of Scripture which again states that the relief of the saints will come on the day of the Lord, which is also called here the day of God. We are to look forward to the day of the Lord (i.e., the rapture) because our relief from tribulation and our rescue from wrath will occur at that time.

Train #6: The Days of Lot and Noah and the Day of the Lord

> But of that day and hour no one knows, not even the angels of heaven, nor the Son, but the Father alone. For the coming of the Son of Man will be just like the days of Noah. For as in those days which were before the flood they were eating and drinking, they were marrying and giving in marriage, until the day that Noah entered the ark, and they did not understand until the flood came and took them all away; **so shall the coming of the Son of Man be** (Matthew 24:36-39).

Look at the specific timing revealed in the following passage:

> . . . but **on the day** that Lot went out from Sodom it rained fire and brimstone from heaven and destroyed them all. **It will be just the same on the day that the Son of Man is revealed** (Luke 17:29-30).

1. Notice that on **the same day** that the Lord is revealed, God's wrath in the form of fire and brimstone will fall. Remember what we just looked at in 2 Peter 3? We are to look forward to that day, for it will also be the time of our rescue. The **same day** that Lot went out from Sodom, it rained fire and brimstone. **It will be the very same** on the day that the Lord is revealed!

Train #7: The Seventh Trumpet and the Harvest

> Behold, I tell you a mystery; we shall not all sleep, but we shall all be changed, in a moment, in the twinkling of an eye, at the **last trumpet;** for the trumpet will sound, and the dead will be raised imperishable, and we shall be changed (1 Corinthians 15:51-52).

> And He will send forth His angels with a **great trumpet** and they will gather together His **elect** from the four winds, from one end of the sky to the other (Matthew 24:31).

> For the Lord Himself will descend from heaven with a shout, with the voice of the archangel, and with the **trumpet** of God; and the dead in Christ shall rise first. Then we who are alive and remain shall be caught up together with them in the clouds to meet the Lord in the air, and thus we shall always be with the Lord (1 Thessalonians 4:16-17).

The things that take place at the seventh trumpet in the book of Revelation match the things that other Scriptures say take place at the harvest, or gathering of the saints, announced by trumpet blast. Let's look again at the description of the happenings at the time of the seventh trumpet:

... but in the days of the voice of the seventh angel, when he is about to sound, then the mystery of God is finished, as He preached to His servants the prophets ... And the seventh angel sounded; and there arose loud voices in heaven, saying, "The kingdom of the world has become the kingdom of our Lord, and of His Christ ... We give Thee thanks, O Lord God, the Almighty, who art and who wast, because Thou has taken Thy great power and hast begun to reign. And the nations were enraged, and **Thy wrath came, and the time came for the dead to be judged, and the time to give their reward to Thy bond-servants the prophets and to the saints and to those who fear Thy name, the small and the great, and to destroy those who destroy the earth."** And the temple of God which is in heaven was opened; and the ark of His covenant appeared in His temple, and there were flashes of lightning and sounds and peals of thunder and an earthquake and a great hailstorm (Revelation 10:7, 11:15, 17-19).

The seventh and last trumpet is the dividing line between what seems to be Phase 1 and Phase 2 of God's wrath. This is the time of the main harvest at the end of Chapter 14, after which we read in the beginning of Chapter 15 about those victorious over the beast in heaven just prior to the pouring out of the final bowls of wrath. The purification of great tribulation has been successful. Those who have endured have been purified and refined into the likeness of Jesus, and they are without spot or wrinkle, ready for the appearance of their Lord.

A Three-phase Harvest?

Jesus said we must endure to the end, to the harvest. The crop harvest in Israel consisted of three natural phases: the first fruits, the main harvest, and the gleanings. The Bible suggests that the Lord will also harvest His crop in the three-phase manner of the historical natural harvests of Israel. This is perhaps the reason why we read about the Lord's appearing in curiously different ways, sometimes like a "thief in the night," and in other places as "every eye shall see Him coming on the clouds." As we focus in closer and closer to the event of the harvest as described in Scripture, we begin to see a broadening of the meaning of the day of the Lord. *Day* in "the day of the Lord" has two meanings: it can mean a specific twenty-four hour day, and it can also mean a longer general period of time. I believe we are seeing both meanings in the Scriptures we are considering.

These seemingly separate events can be reconciled if we consider the harvest of the elect as a three-phase harvest of three separate events, both in terms of time and the nature of those harvested. The Bible describes a first-fruits harvest at the beginning of Chapter 14 and a main harvest at the end of Chapter 14. A gleanings harvest is not so readily apparent. However, there is a curious parenthetical statement at the sixth bowl, **"Behold, I am coming like a thief . . ."** I believe this statement identifies the harvest of the gleanings.

The rewarded Church also seems to be described as a three-some. These are the bondservants the prophets, the saints, and those who fear His name.

> And the nations were enraged, and Thy wrath came, and the time came for the dead to be judged, and the time to give their reward to Thy bond-servants the prophets **and** to the saints **and** to those who fear Thy name, the small and the great, and to destroy those who destroy the earth (Revelation 11:18).

Bondservants in general may correspond to those taken at the harvest of the first fruits. *The saints* may correspond to those taken in the main harvest. *Those who fear Thy name* may correspond to those taken at the harvest of the gleanings. In no way do I hold to these things absolutely. I am only suggesting a model which seems to explain some of these things. We must hold loosely the things which the Lord has not revealed absolutely.

Tentative Benchmark #10: The Main Harvest is Associated with "Coming on the Clouds" and Every Eye Seeing Him

... and then the sign of the Son of Man will appear in the sky, and then all the tribes of the earth will mourn, and they will see the SON OF MAN COMING ON THE CLOUDS OF THE SKY with power and great glory. And He will send forth His angels with A GREAT TRUMPET and THEY WILL GATHER TOGETHER His elect from the four winds, from one end of the sky to the other (Matthew 24:30-31).

BEHOLD, HE IS COMING WITH THE CLOUDS, and every eye will see Him, even those who pierced Him; and all the tribes of the earth will mourn over Him. Even so. Amen (Revelation 1:7).

And I looked, and behold, a white cloud, and SITTING ON A CLOUD WAS ONE LIKE A SON OF MAN, having a golden crown on His head, and a sharp sickle in His hand. And another angel came out of the temple, crying out with a loud voice to Him who sat on the cloud, "Put in your sickle and reap, because the hour to reap has come, because the **harvest** of the earth is ripe." And He who sat on the cloud swung His sickle over the earth; and the earth was reaped (Revelation 14:14-16).

These passages seem consistent in identifying the "coming in the clouds" with the main harvest taking place at the seventh and last trumpet.

Tentative Benchmark #11: The Gleaning Harvest is Associated with "Coming Like a Thief"

After the harvest of the wheat comes the harvest of the grapes. Yet there are apparently still a few stalks of wheat left in the harvest fields who will have witnessed the main harvest and be converted as they continue to witness and experience the terror of the events immediately following in the form of the world-wide bowl judgments. Those who see these things are told to fear God and give Him glory. I believe those who do are saved. Many will disagree. But I believe the redemptive heart of God is not willing that any should perish. He will provide the offer of salvation up until the literal twenty-four hour day of the Lord which corresponds to Lot coming out of Sodom on the day that fire and brimstone fell. Lot was deemed a righteous man, but he escaped on the very last day, at the very last moment.

> And another angel came out of the temple which is in heaven, and he also had a sharp sickle. And another angel, the one who has power over fire, came out from the altar; and he called with a loud voice to him who had the sharp sickle, saying, "Put in your sharp sickle, and gather the clusters from the vine of the earth, because her grapes are ripe." And the angel swung his sickle to the earth, and gathered the clusters from the vine of the earth, and threw them into the great wine press of the wrath of God. And the wine press was trodden outside the city, and blood came out from the wine press, up to the horses' bridles, for a distance of two hundred miles (Revelation 14:17-20).

If the main harvest of wheat takes place at the seventh trumpet, then gleanings by definition must take place afterwards. But all that remains after the seventh trumpet are the bowls of wrath. If the harvest model is applicable, then we should find evidence of a gleaning harvest somewhere mixed in with the bowl judgments.

Just before the outpouring of the seventh and final bowl comes the curious parenthetical statement of Revelation 16:15, **"Behold, I am coming like a thief. Blessed is the one who stays awake and keeps his garments, lest he walk about naked and men see his shame."** Is this a reference back to an earlier event, or does it mean that Jesus is coming like a thief right here between the sixth and seventh bowls? The plain sense of Scripture is that a separation takes place at this point which results in some being taken to the place called Har-Magedon.

> And I saw coming out of the mouth of the dragon and out of the mouth of the beast and out of the mouth of the false prophet, three unclean spirits like frogs; for they are

spirits of demons, performing signs, which go out to the kings of the whole world, to gather them together for the **war of the great day of God,** the Almighty. **("Behold, I am coming like a thief. Blessed is the one who stays awake and keeps his garments, lest he walk about naked and men see his shame.")** And they gathered them together to the place which in Hebrew is called Har-Magedon. And the seventh angel poured out his bowl upon the air; and a loud voice came out of the temple from the throne, saying, "It is done" (Revelation 16:13-17).

I believe this reference to "coming like a thief" includes the harvesting of the gleanings on the same twenty-four hour day that the final wrath of God will fall. Let's consider once again these familiar passages:

But immediately after the tribulation of those days the sun will be darkened, and the moon will not give its light, and the stars will fall from the sky, and the powers of the heavens will be shaken, and then the sign of the Son of Man will appear in the sky, and then all the tribes of the earth will mourn, and they will see the Son of Man coming on the clouds of the sky with power and great glory. And He will send forth His angels with a great trumpet and they will gather together His elect from the four winds, from one end of the sky to the other. Now learn the parable from the fig tree; when its branch has already become tender, and puts forth its leaves, you know that summer is near; even so you, too, when you see **all these things,** recognize that **He is near, right at the door** (Matthew 24:29-33).

Even so you, too, when you see **all these things,** recognize that He is near, right at the door. And one of these things which we will see is Jesus in the clouds sending His angels to harvest the wheat. Every eye will see Him. These Scriptures seem to say that when that happens, He is **still at the door.** If He is still at the door, when does He come back? He seems to come back in Revelation 19:11, which I believe is a more detailed description of the grape harvest. **The treading of the grapes does not take place until Jesus returns to the earth, for it is on earth that the treading will take place!** Jesus does not have to come to earth to harvest His wheat. That harvesting is done by angels that He sends as He watches from His seat in the clouds, **right at the door!** Then, on the specific twenty-four hour day of the Lord, the day of His return, the day of the harvest of the gleanings, the very day on which the earth and all things on it will be destroyed, **He is revealed and He comes!** In between the main harvest and the harvest of the gleanings is an uncertain length of time, perhaps thirty days. During this time the wedding supper of the Lamb in heaven, the mourning of remnant Israel on earth, and the pouring out of the bowls of wrath may take place. This would seem to be the point at which Jesus returns to rescue Israel from the nations who have gathered against Jerusalem.

> And I saw heaven opened; and behold, a white horse, and He who sat upon it is called Faithful and True; and in righteousness He judges and wages war. And His eyes are a flame of fire, and upon His head are many diadems; and He has a name written upon Him which no one knows except Himself. And He is clothed with a robe dipped in blood; and His name is called The Word of God. And the armies which are in heaven, clothed in fine linen, white and clean, were following Him on white horses. And from His mouth comes a sharp sword, so that with it He may smite the nations; and He will rule them with a rod of iron; and He treads the wine press of the fierce wrath of God, the Almighty. And on His robe and on His thigh He has a name written, "KING OF KINGS, AND LORD OF LORDS" (Revelation 19:11-16).

> ... but on **the day** that Lot went out from Sodom it rained fire and brimstone from heaven and destroyed them all. It will be **just the same on the day that the Son of Man is revealed** ... I tell you, on **that night** there will be two men in one bed; one will be taken, and the other will be left. There will be two women grinding at the same place; one will be taken, and the other will be left. (Two men will be in the field; one will be taken and the other will be left.) And answering they said to Him, "Where, Lord?" And He said to them, "Where the body is, there also will the vultures be gathered" (Luke 17:29-30, 34-37).

A Possible Scenario of the Last Days and the Return of the Lord

Remember, this is a *possible scenario*, not an absolute one. I don't claim to know these absolute details. I only know what I believe Scripture says, and I am trying to piece together a possible and feasible scenario given existing Scripture. Please do not be turned off by disagreement with these details. Please do not throw the rest of the book away because you do not agree with these details. No two of us on the planet agree with all these details. We all see through a glass with various shades of darkness. But I'm going to plod ahead as far as I can. I don't want to present mere speculation here, but at the same time I want to share with you what seems sensible to me. I think we all have a little piece of the puzzle — what the Lord has given each of us. If we can put all our pieces together, maybe we can see a bit further than if we keep it all to ourselves. No one is going to figure this out to the day or the hour, for Scripture says we will **all** be surprised when He comes back. But have we pushed it yet to the point beyond which we cannot know? God will be pleased if we push it right up to that point, for the seeking out of these things pleases Him. I received a prophetic word one day that God was pleased with the study I was doing. The man who gave it had no idea I was seeking these things out. It was a great joy to realize that God is pleased when we struggle to understand these things.

> It is the glory of God to conceal a matter, but the glory of kings is to search out a matter (Proverbs 25:2).

We are all kings, and we have been given specific times to ponder. We are told that the sixth trumpet ends at about the 1260-day point. We are told in the book of Daniel that there will be 1290 days, and blessed is the one who waits until the 1335th day. It would seem that the seventh trumpet, the harvest of the saints, all of the seven bowls of God's wrath, and the return of our Lord will all be concentrated in these final seventy-five days. We know the redeemed nation of Israel will mourn for the One they have pierced, and the traditional period of mourning in the Bible was thirty days.

Also, the sequence of the Feast of Tabernacles undoubtedly fits in here somewhere.

> And in that day His feet will stand on the Mount of Olives . . . For it will be a unique day which is known to the LORD, neither day nor night, but it will come about that at evening time there will be light . . . And the LORD will be king over all the earth; in that day the LORD will be the only one, and His name the only one . . . Then it will come about that any who are left of all the nations that went against Jerusalem will go up from year to year to worship the King, the LORD of hosts, and to celebrate the Feast of Booths (Zechariah 14:4, 7, 9, 16).

As I read through Zechariah Chapters 12-14, I get the distinct impression that the celebration of the Feast of Booths (or Feast of Tabernacles) that the Lord orders for all nations may commemorate His return. The Feast of Booths begins on the fifteenth day of the seventh month. Let's consider for a moment that it could line up with the 1335th day that we are told to wait for in the book of Daniel. **"How blessed is he who keeps waiting and attains to the 1335 days!"** We know that the 1260-day point is the end of the sixth trumpet. The one big event that must fall between the 1260-day point and the 1335-day point would then be the harvest at the seventh trumpet. Will that be on the 1290th day? **"And from the time that the regular sacrifice is abolished, and the abomination of desolation is set up, there will be 1290 days."**

The end that Daniel is being told about involves the rescuing of his people and the resurrection of the dead which we know takes place at the main harvest when the living and dead join Jesus in the clouds. Scripture indicates that the nation of Israel will see Him return for the harvest, but they will mourn for the One they have pierced and for having missed the harvest.

> Harvest is past, summer is ended, and we are not saved. For the brokenness of the daughter of my people I am broken; I mourn, dismay has taken hold of me (Jeremiah 8:20-21).

"And it will come about in that day," declares the Lord GOD, "that I shall make the sun go down at noon and make the earth dark in broad daylight . . . And I will make it like a time of mourning for an only son, and the end of it will be like a bitter day" (Amos 8:9-10).

Behold, He is coming with the clouds, and every eye will see Him, even those who pierced Him; and all the tribes of the earth will mourn over Him. Even so. Amen (Revelation 1:7).

And I will pour out on the house of David and on the inhabitants of Jerusalem, the Spirit of grace and of supplication, so that they will look on Me whom they have pierced; and they will mourn for Him, as one mourns for an only son, and they will weep bitterly over Him, like the bitter weeping over a first-born (Zechariah 12:10).

If that period of mourning following the harvest at the 1290-day point should be the historical thirty days, that would bring us to the 1320-day point. There would then be fifteen days for the Feast of Ingathering to be fulfilled, which takes place after the main harvest and the crops have been gathered in. On the first day of the Feast of Ingathering is the blowing of trumpets to call the people. God supernaturally delivered His people out of Egypt. Scripture is clear that He will supernaturally deliver the remnant of Israel out of the nations and regather them to Jerusalem.

It will come about also in that day that a great trumpet will be blown; and those who were perishing in the land of Assyria and who were scattered in the land of Egypt will come and worship the LORD in the holy mountain at Jerusalem (Isaiah 27:13).

On the tenth day of the Feast of Ingathering is the day of atonement. The Bible indicates that God will remove the sins of Israel in one day.

"For behold, the stone that I have set before Joshua; on one stone are seven eyes. Behold I will engrave an inscription on it," declares the LORD of hosts, "and **I will remove the iniquity of that land in one day.** In that day," declares the Lord of hosts, "every one of you will invite his neighbor to sit under his vine and under his fig tree" (Zechariah 3:9-10).

On the fifteenth day begins the Feast of Booths or Tabernacles. If this should coincide with the physical return of the Lord to Jerusalem, it would fit with all nations being ordered to ever after commemorate the Feast of Tabernacles by going up to Jerusalem. Traditionally the last day of this feast is a time of great rejoicing and gaiety in Jewish households world-wide. What greater reason for joy and rejoicing could there be than the return of their long-awaited Messiah, the Lord Jesus Christ!

And Yet . . . No One Knows

>For the coming of the Son of Man will be just like the days of Noah. For as in those days which were before the flood they were eating and drinking, they were marrying and giving in marriage, until the day that Noah entered the ark, and they did not understand until the flood came and took them all away; so shall the coming of the Son of Man be. Then there will be two men in the field; one will be taken, and one will be left. Two women will be grinding at the mill; one will be taken, and one will be left. Therefore be on the alert, for **YOU DO NOT KNOW WHICH DAY YOUR LORD IS COMING** (Matthew 24:37-42).

>But be sure of this, that if the head of the house had known at what time of the night the thief was coming, he would have been on the alert and would not have allowed his house to be broken into. For this reason you be ready too; for **THE SON OF MAN IS COMING AT AN HOUR WHEN YOU DO NOT THINK HE WILL** (Matthew 24:43-44).

>But of that day and hour **no one knows,** not even the angels of heaven, nor the Son, but the Father alone (Matthew 24:36).

But the Point is . . .

I don't want to spend any more time on these uncertain details because that is not the purpose of this book. The one thing we do know with certainty, and the main point this chapter is trying to make, is that the main harvest of the Church is consistently portrayed as near or at the end of the final seven years of the age, somewhere between day 1260 and day 1335. God's people are seen to be protected through the first stages of His wrath, and removed from the earth before His final wrath is poured out. The exact details are not given. We can know generally but not specifically. We can know what we need to know. We are called to endure to the harvest at the end of the age, and that is consistently taught by the numerous scriptural examples we have studied.

We must at this point reaffirm the primary call of the Church at the end of the age, initially presented in the book of Daniel and expanded upon in the book of Revelation, as a call to endurance to the harvest at the end of the age or to martyrdom. This is such a difficult cup to consider that little teaching exists along this line. We have seen that the great multitude that no one could count at the sixth seal is most likely not a great multitude of raptured saints as we might have wished, but rather a great multitude of martyred saints, who underscore by their numbers the primacy of the call of martyrdom for the Church at the end of the age. Those who will be raptured are referred to as "those of us who are alive and remain," as if these will be a minority rather than a majority.

The physical overcoming of the saints as initially revealed in the book of Daniel and upheld throughout the book of Revelation is a primary means by which Satan is overcome and ultimately defeated by a Church created for that very purpose. The purpose of God to demonstrate His wisdom through the Church to the rulers and authorities in the heavenly places rests on the foundation of that wisdom being the cross of Jesus Christ. It was initially demonstrated through His Son and will again be demonstrated at the end of the age through the corporate body of His Son. No higher call is possible; no greater destiny lies before us than the laying down of earthly life for the accomplishment of this primary purpose for His Church. Let us rise to embrace this call. We must grow in our love for God's glory.

For those mothers who are fearful for their sons or daughters, be comforted in that the Father's call for your sons and daughters is of infinite eternal love. This love is most represented in His children by the laying down of their lives for others. Greater love has no one than this. I expect you will want your children ultimately to rise to embrace that level of love and testimony if so called. For the eternal joy set beyond for you and your children, be comforted and be at rest in your Father's arms. Our lives upon this earth are only a passing shadow. Be comforted in anticipation of the joy that awaits us for all eternity.

"Father, we no longer want to seek our own glory. Give us a holy love for Your glory. Change our hearts to conform with the issues of Your Heart. Father, give us grace to embrace Your plan for Your Church at the end of the age. We cry out to be shaped and fired as vessels to be used for noble purposes. Please don't let us fall short! Do whatever it takes to keep us on the right path. Choose our footsteps, Father, and keep us from falling away. We desperately need Your grace to stand in these times ahead! Father, hear the cries of our hearts! We want to glorify You with our lives and with our deaths! Help us, Father, to finish our races well! We must stand before You to hear, 'Well done, good and faithful servants.' No lesser evaluation is acceptable! Help us! Help us, Father! Pour out Your grace upon Your Church in order that we may be vessels found noble to demonstrate Your wisdom to the rulers and authorities in the heavenly places at the end of this age! Amen."

PART THREE

Identification of Key Groups

ELEVEN

Who are the Two Witnesses?

Are these two really Moses and Elijah, or are they a corporate body of the Church? The intent of this chapter is to define their witness as the ultimate witness of the Church at the end of the age, and also to excite the Church about praying for the possibility of being included as part of this witness company. But regardless of who they are and how many there are, there is much to be learned from their ministry that impacts the vision and calling of the entire Church at the end of the age.

> And I will grant authority to **my two witnesses,** and they will prophesy for twelve hundred and sixty days, clothed in sackcloth. These are the two olive trees and the two lampstands that stand before the Lord of the earth (Revelation 11:3-4).

Standing before the Lord of the earth identifies them as the Lord's witnesses, and the voice saying "I will grant authority to my two witnesses" must then be the voice of the Lord. They are the Lord's witnesses and therefore a part of His Church, regardless of who they are. Their witness is a demonstration of the Church at the end of the age operating in the full power and authority of Jesus Christ. Nevertheless, they are physically overcome by the power of Satan. But, as we have seen, that is the primary call of the saints at the end of the age. The ultimate demonstration of power and authority at the end of the age will be evidenced by the wisdom of the cross of Jesus Christ which crushes Satan underfoot.

Jesus told His disciples that **they** would be **His** witnesses when they had received power from the Holy Spirit. Their ministry was then to begin in Jerusalem and extend to all of Judea, to Samaria, and then to the remotest parts of the world. We are in the days of witnessing to the remotest parts of the world. We can only be His witnesses when we receive power from the Holy Spirit, and to the extent we have not received that power, we cannot be His witnesses. At the three and one-half year point of the final seven years of the age, in Revelation Chapter 12:10, there is indication of a great outpouring of power from the Holy Spirit. It is this outpouring of the Spirit that will empower the final thrust of world evangelism and trigger the beginning of the witness period of 1260 days of the two witnesses.

> And I heard a loud voice in heaven, saying, "Now the salvation, and the power, and the kingdom of our God and the authority of His Christ have come, for the accuser of our brethren has been thrown down, who accuses them before our God day and night" (Revelation 12:10).

> And this gospel of the kingdom shall be preached in the whole world for a witness to all the nations, and then the end shall come (Matthew 24:14).

> And I saw another angel flying in midheaven, having an eternal gospel to preach to those who live on the earth, and to every nation and tribe and tongue and people . . . (Revelation 14:6).

I believe Scripture indicates there will be another day of first fruits/Pentecost much like the first day in Acts 2. And I believe, as a result, the last three and one-half years of this age are going to be much like Acts 2 only more so. The prophecies of Joel are yet to be fully realized. The evidence of the new day of Pentecost will be the gathering of the first fruits of Revelation 14:4 and the falling of the Holy Spirit in great power and authority as described in Revelation 12:10. The male child is caught up to heaven; and the remainder of the wheat harvest, left on earth to ripen until Revelation 14:14, is anointed with great power and authority in order to overcome Satan by the Blood of the Lamb, the word of their testimony, and by loving not their lives unto death. Here, at the three and one-half year point before the end of the age, is the start of the period of witness of the two witnesses in power and authority in demonstration of the Spirit poured out without measure.

I believe that once again all nations, tribes, tongues and peoples may hear the gospel preached in their native tongues without the benefit of translators. The messengers of Revelation 14:6, having the eternal gospel to preach to every nation, tribe, tongue, and people, will be speaking in tongues that all peoples can understand. The shadows of the saints will once again heal the sick. But once again, Ananiases and Sapphiras will drop dead from words out of the mouths of the witnesses of Jesus. Along with great power will come great requirement.

The 1260-day witness period of the two witnesses in power and authority ends with their death at the hands of the beast from the abyss, followed by their resurrection from the dead three and one-half days later. This is the first revelation from the little book of Daniel reopened in the hands of the angel in Revelation 10:2.

> "But as for you, Daniel, conceal these words and seal up the book until the end of time; many will go back and forth, and knowledge will increase." Then I, Daniel, looked and behold, two others were standing, one on this bank of the river, and the other on that bank of the river. And one said to the man dressed in linen, who was above the waters of the river, "How long will it be until the end of these wonders?" And I heard the man dressed in linen, who was above the waters of the river, as he raised his right hand and his left toward heaven, and swore by Him who lives forever that it would be for a time, times, and half a time [1260 days or three and one-half years]; and as

soon as they finish **shattering the power of the holy people,** all these events will be completed. As for me, I heard but could not understand; so I said, "My lord, what will be the outcome of these events?" And he said, "Go your way, Daniel, for these words are concealed and sealed up until the end time" (Daniel 12:4-9).

We see in Revelation 11:7 the shattering of the power of at least two holy people at the end of a specific time period of 1260 days. Who are these two ultimate witnesses? Are the holy people of Daniel 12:7 represented here by only two individuals, or are they a corporate group of prophetic saints?

And so when they had come together, they were asking Him, saying, "Lord, is it at this time You are restoring the kingdom to Israel?" He said to them, "It is not for you to know times or epochs which the Father has fixed by His own authority; but you shall receive power when the Holy Spirit has come upon you; and **you shall be My witnesses** both in Jerusalem, and in all Judea and Samaria, and even to the remotest part of the earth" (Acts 1:6-8).

This prophecy of Jesus is not applicable to only two individuals, but to the entire body of Christ. We are all to be His witnesses. But are we to be **these** witnesses?

Moses and Elijah?

There is much interpretation that the two witnesses of Revelation 11 are Moses and Elijah or some other combination of Old Testament saints. But Ephesians 3:9-10 says that it is through the Church of Jesus Christ that God will demonstrate His wisdom to the rulers and authorities in the heavenly places. Why would the ultimate witness at the end of the age not be the living corporate Church? I am uneasy with the *Moses and Elijah* interpretation because it establishes a *not us* but *them* mentality, when it was to His Church that Jesus said, **"You will be My witnesses."**

The Lampstands are the Churches

> ... and the seven lampstands are the seven churches (Revelation 1:20).

> These are the two olive trees and the two lampstands that stand before the Lord of the earth (Revelation 11:4).

The term *lampstand*, which also identifies each of the seven churches in Revelation 1:20, is a strong indicator that these two witnesses represent at least some of the Church. They are warred against and physically overcome by the beast during the last three and one-half years of the age, even as the saints are warred against and overcome by the beast during the last three and one-half years of the age. And even as the saints emerge victorious after being overcome, so do these two witnesses emerge victorious from being overcome as they are resurrected to heaven after lying dead for three and one-half days. They serve as a precise fulfillment of the prophecies in Daniel in which the holy and powerful people will be warred against, physically overcome, and yet emerge victorious as recipients of the Kingdom.

Individual or Corporate?

How many olives does an olive tree bear? Olive trees and lampstands suggest more than two individuals. There is also a hint of corporateness in that they are warred against. War is usually fought against more that two individuals.

There is also a suggestion of corporateness in Revelation 11:8-9 which identifies their dead bodies as lying in the street of **"the great city"** and that **"those from the peoples and tribes and tongues and nations will look at their dead bodies..."**

Bodies or Images of Bodies?

Modern technology allows a ready interpretation of this viewing of their bodies, but the text does not say that peoples and tribes and tongues and nations will look at *images* of their bodies, as one might expect if they were on world-wide telecast. The term *image* is used elsewhere in the book regarding the false prophet (who creates an image of the beast), so the use of image here would be appropriate if it were applicable. Could the reason that peoples, tribes, tongues, and nations look upon their bodies, and not upon *images* of their bodies, be because their bodies are everywhere to be looked upon while lying in the streets of the great cities of Babylon? The margin notes of my study Bible indicate that in some manuscripts, it is their *body* rather than their *bodies* that lie in the streets. That opens up the possibility of a *body* of believers. In the following passage, the woman, the great city of Babylon, is drunk with the blood of the witnesses of Jesus.

> . . . and upon her forehead a name was written, a mystery, "BABYLON THE GREAT, THE MOTHER OF HARLOTS AND OF THE ABOMINATIONS OF THE EARTH." And I saw the woman **drunk with the blood of the saints, and with the blood of the witnesses of Jesus.** And when I saw her, I wondered greatly. And the angel said to me, "Why do you wonder? I shall tell you the mystery of the woman and of the beast that carries her, which has the seven heads and the ten horns . . . And the woman whom you saw is the **great city,** which reigns over the kings of the earth" (Revelation 17:5-7, 18).

Great City or Holy City?

Jerusalem is referred to as the *holy city* in Revelation 11:2. The term *great city* is used consistently throughout the book of Revelation as a reference to the unholy city of Babylon. A simultaneous world-wide killing of Jesus' witnesses is conceivable because Scripture indicates that multiple images of the beast will have been set up seemingly world-wide that must be worshiped in order to avoid death. The technology to kill vast numbers of people through computer and satellite technology is at hand. However, Satan may not need to rely on the technology of man to accomplish his work. He will not be restricted in his use of power at the end of the age by what man has engineered. Nor will the witnesses of Jesus.

> And their dead bodies [body] will lie in the street of the **great city** which mystically is called Sodom and Egypt, where also their Lord was crucified. And those from the peoples and tribes and tongues and nations will look at their dead bodies [body] for three and a half days, and will not permit their dead bodies to be laid in a tomb (Revelation 11:8-9).

Why doesn't Scripture just come right out and say that their bodies will lie in the streets of Jerusalem if Jerusalem is where they will lie? I think this terminology opens up the possibility that these streets are other than the streets of Jerusalem. In a spiritual sense, I believe the following Scripture indicates the Blood of Jesus is also found in the great city of Babylon, even though He was crucified in Jerusalem, although technically **outside** of the city gates.

> And in her [the great city of Babylon] was found the blood of prophets and of saints and of **ALL** who have been slain on the earth (Revelation 18:24).

A Glimpse of the Church having Arrived!

Regardless of who they are and where they will lie, this is a snapshot of the Church operating in the full power and authority of Jesus Christ. These two witnesses are described as doing even greater things than Jesus did, as He said those who believed in Him would do. As difficult as it may be to positively relate these two witnesses to two larger corporate bodies, there are many prophecies to the Church fulfilled by these two — be they two individuals or corporate. If there are only two individuals who gain this stature, then let each of us who desires the greater gift of prophecy and such a ministry seek to be one of them. If there are more than two, our prayers will still be valid.

What greater prophetic calling exists than to be one of these two witnesses at the end of the age? Should our response be any different whether there are two or two million of them? This is a description of the ultimate destiny of the Church on earth: to walk in the fullness of the power and authority of Jesus Christ, and to lay down our lives as testimony. It is by the Blood of the Lamb, the word of our testimony, and by loving not our lives unto death that we are destined to overcome Satan.

A Corporate *One New Man* of Jew and Gentile?

The mystery of the overcoming Church, as revealed by Paul in Ephesians Chapters 2 and 3, is that it will be made up of two groups — Jew and Gentile — reconciled into one by the cross of Jesus Christ. It is **this** Church and **only this** Church that will allow the demonstration of God's wisdom to the rulers and authorities in the heavenly places (Ephesians 3:10). A divided Church or a Church that is not composed of a unity of Jew and Gentile will not allow it.

> Therefore, He will give them up until the time when she who is in labor has borne a child. Then the remainder of His brethren will return to the sons of Israel (Micah 5:3).

Whatever this means, it matches the *she* who bears a child in Revelation Chapter 12 at the three and one-half year point before the end of the age. Perhaps it is at this time that the remainder of His brethren return to the sons of Israel and the two become one new man. Perhaps it is at this time that the two physical witnesses — Jew and Gentile — can represent the spiritual one-new-man Church that will allow the demonstration of the wisdom of God to the rulers and authorities during the last three and one-half years of the age. They are physically two, but spiritually one new man.

Two Olive Trees and Two Lampstands

We cannot avoid concluding that the two witnesses represent at least a portion of the Church operating in the full power and authority of Jesus Christ. Israel is referred to in Scripture as a cultivated olive tree, while Gentiles are referred to as a wild olive tree. Together they are reconciled in one body, out of a common root, to God through the cross (Ephesians 2:16). Could this be the model for the two witnesses? Together they stand as two physical olive trees and two lampstands before the Lord demonstrating God's wisdom through a spiritually united Church to the rulers and authorities during the last three and one-half years of the age.

> For if you [Gentiles] were cut off from what is by nature a wild olive tree, and were grafted contrary to nature into a cultivated olive tree [Jew], how much more shall these who are the natural branches be grafted into their own olive tree? (Romans 11:24).

Whether they are two or two million, they represent the finest wine of the end-time Church. As powerful as they are, however, they are not as physically powerful as Satan. Victory at the end of the age will not be decided on the basis of physical power. The race is not to the swift or the battle to the strong, but to God. And His wisdom is the wisdom of the cross. As we choose to embrace the cross in absolute weakness, His wisdom will be demonstrated through us, and Satan will be crushed underfoot.

Elijah Who is to Come

I believe these two witnesses do indeed represent Elijah who is to come. They are not a resurrected Elijah, but a corporate body in the spirit and power of Elijah. These are among those upon whom the Lord has poured out His Spirit without measure as described in Revelation 12:10. These are, at least in part, those who will overcome Satan by the Blood of the Lamb, by the word of their testimony, and by loving not their lives unto death. These are, at least in part, the last-days Church operating in the fullness of Jesus' power and authority. This has to be a description of the finest wine and the greater glory of the latter house. These are the recipients of the deluge of the latter rain that will walk this earth as the greatest witness for Jesus Christ the world has ever or will ever see. This is Acts 2 but even more so. These are those that all creation has been waiting to see revealed on earth. This is the fullness of the representation of Jesus Christ living in and through His people.

Them or Us?

I want to move these two witnesses from being *them* to the realm of possibility of being *us*. They are the Lord's witnesses and therefore members of His Church. I don't believe it will be part of the plan to bring specific Old Testament personalities into the end-times picture. Scripture states that it is through the Church, a corporate body of Jew and Gentile, that God will demonstrate His wisdom to the rulers and authorities in the heavenly places at the end of the age. It is upon the rock of the revelation of Jesus Christ that the Church is built. Nor are they the whole Church, because not everyone in the Church is going to be a bondservant and a prophet. There are at least three sub-groupings in the Church separately identified as bondservants, saints, and those who fear God's name. These are a portion of the Church called to a specific prophetic role, and I suggest they may be more than two unique individuals. I want to leave you with a desire to be one of them, for we are all told to eagerly seek the gift of prophecy.

If there are only two of them, so be it. In any case, they are the definers of the vision for the rest of the Church and establish the nature of the race we are called to run. This is the direction our prayers should take and these are the greater deeds that we should pray to be doing at the end of the age, for the anointing of the Holy Spirit will be poured out upon all flesh according to Scripture. When all is said and done, if we have not, it will have been because we asked not.

The Holy Spirit indicated, during a hot and heavy sense of His presence one day, that the anointing available was to the extent of *Su Koros*, which translates from the Greek to *thy measure*. Truly the measure available to each of us is *thy measure*. Let our measures be *without measure* even as was Jesus' measure of the fullness of the Holy Spirit. Let us not *have not* because we asked not. Won't it be interesting if we find that the number of these witnesses operating in this extent of power and authority was up to us? These are people of choice, as they have been given power and authority to smite the earth with every plague as often as they desire. What do we desire?

TWELVE

Who are the Woman and Her Children?

And a great sign appeared in heaven: a woman clothed with the sun, and the moon under her feet, and on her head a crown of twelve stars; and she was with child; and she cried out, being in labor and in pain to give birth. And another sign appeared in heaven: and behold, a great red dragon having seven heads and ten horns, and on his heads were seven diadems. And his tail swept away a third of the stars of heaven, and threw them to the earth. And the dragon stood before the woman who was about to give birth, so that when she gave birth, he might devour her child. **And she gave birth to a son, a male child,** who is to rule all the nations with a rod of iron; and her child was caught up to God and to His throne. And the woman fled into the wilderness where she had a place prepared by God, so that there she might be nourished for one thousand two hundred and sixty days (Revelation 12:1-6).

And when the dragon saw that he was thrown down to the earth, he persecuted the woman who gave birth to the male child. And the two wings of the great eagle were given to the woman, in order that she might fly into the wilderness to her place, where she was nourished for a time and times and half a time, from the presence of the serpent. And the serpent poured water like a river out of his mouth after the woman, so that he might cause her to be swept away with the flood. And the earth helped the woman, and the earth opened its mouth and drank up the river which the dragon poured out of his mouth. And the dragon was enraged with the woman, and went off to make war with the **rest of her offspring, who keep the commandments of God and hold to the testimony of Jesus** (Revelation 12:13-17).

This is perhaps the most mysterious and yet foundational vision in the Bible concerning God's plan for the outworking of the redemption of His creation at the end of the age. Identifying the woman and her children is crucial to understanding the makeup of the company of the redeemed. The whole of prophetic Scripture must be considered in order to arrive at an identification of these key players. She is revealed in heaven as a great sign along with her children, the "male child" and the "rest of her offspring." Who or what are they a sign of, and can these heavenly signs be matched with flesh and blood counterparts on earth?

It is easy to see that this heavenly vision has application to the entire history of the redeemed line. Since the time of Eve, there has always been a *woman* struggling to give birth, and the devil has always sought to kill her offspring. The application to Moses and Jesus, and the situation with Esther and Haman, come to mind. Yet we are challenged and constrained here with identifying a particular segment of the overall vision which applies specifically to the last three and one-half years of the age. In other words, who are the people groups on earth during the last three and one-half years of the age who represent the subjects of this heavenly vision?

Who are the "Rest of her Offspring"?

The first and easiest match that can be made is the ready match between the "rest of her offspring" that the dragon goes off to make war against, with the saints of Daniel and Revelation.

And the dragon was enraged with the woman, and went off to make war with the **rest of her offspring,** who keep the commandments of God and hold to the testimony of Jesus (Revelation 12:17).

And it was given to him [the antichrist] to make war with the **saints and to overcome them;** and authority over every tribe and people and tongue and nation was given to him (Revelation 13:7).

We have already concluded that these saints represent the final generation Church on earth at the end of the age. Revelation Chapters 13 and 14 describe that war between Satan and the saints. Throughout, the saints are encouraged to keep their perseverance and faith (Revelation 13:10), and to keep the commandments of God and their faith in Jesus (Revelation 14:12). Authority over every tribe and people and tongue and nation is given to the antichrist; but a great multitude that no one could count, from every tribe and people and tongue and nation, emerges victoriously from that war.

Who is the Male Child?

The description of the male child so much resembles Jesus that it is difficult to tell if the vision is referring to Jesus of two thousand years ago or to the overcoming Church, for the overcoming Church will also rule the nations with a rod of iron.

Scholars have different opinions. Most conclude the ready analogy to Jesus, yet Scripture indicates a birth at the three and one-half year point before the end of the age that signifies something other than the birth of Jesus two thousand years ago. Jesus likened the events just preceding the end of the age to increasing birth pains. Someone is going to be birthed at the end of the age, but who is it?

Paul said that the whole creation is groaning as in the pains of childbirth for the revealing of the sons of God. The birth of the male child, the only birth clearly identified in the book of Revelation, suggests that this male child might have something to do with those sons of God for which the whole creation is waiting.

> And she gave birth to a son, a male child, who is to rule all the nations with a rod of iron; and her child was caught up to God and to His throne. And the woman fled into the wilderness where she had a place prepared by God, so that there she might be nourished for one thousand two hundred and sixty days (Revelation 12:5-6).

> I will surely tell of the decree of the LORD: He said to me, "Thou art My Son, today I have begotten Thee. Ask of Me, and I will surely give the nations as Thine inheritance, and the very ends of the earth as Thy possession. Thou shalt break them with a rod of iron, Thou shalt shatter them like earthenware" (Psalm 2:7-9).

> And he who overcomes, and he who keeps My deeds **until the end**, to him I will give authority over the nations; and he shall rule them with a rod of iron, as the vessels of the potter are broken to pieces, as I also have received authority from My Father . . . (Revelation 2:26-27).

> Because you have kept the word of My perseverance, I also will keep you from the hour of testing, that hour which is about to come upon the whole world, to test those who dwell upon the earth . . . He who overcomes, I will make him a pillar in the temple of My God, and he will not go out from it anymore; and I will write upon him the name of My God, and the name of the city of My God, the new Jerusalem, which comes down out of heaven from My God, and My new name. He who has an ear, let him hear what the Spirit says to the churches (Revelation 3:10, 12-13).

> Be on guard, that your hearts may not be weighted down with dissipation and drunkenness and the worries of life, and that day come on you suddenly like a trap; for it will come upon all those who dwell on the face of all the earth. But keep on the alert at all times, **praying** in order that you may have strength to escape [be accounted worthy to escape, KJV] all these things that are about to

take place, and to stand before the Son of Man (Luke 21:34-36).

And I looked, and behold, the Lamb was standing on Mount Zion, and with Him one hundred and forty-four thousand, having His name and the name of His Father written on their foreheads . . . These are the ones who have not been defiled with women, for they have kept themselves chaste. These are the ones who follow the Lamb wherever He goes. These have been purchased **from among men** as first fruits to God and to the Lamb. And no lie was found in their mouth; they are blameless (Revelation 14:1, 4-5).

The male child is best represented as a select group of Jewish and Gentile Church overcomers who have ripened early into the likeness of Jesus and are taken to heaven at the mid-point of the final seven years of the age. This is not the whole Church, but only a first-fruits portion representing the eventual greater harvest. These are blameless saints who have no need of further testing and purification by the fires of tribulation. The timing and description of the male child snatched up to heaven at the beginning of the final three and one-half years of the age matches the timing of the appearance and the description of the 144,000 before God's throne of Revelation 14:1.

If the number 144,000 is literal, and if there are nominally two billion Christians on earth at the end of the age, the ratio selected would only be approximately one in twenty thousand, assuming that the dead in Christ are not involved. Even as the ratio of first fruits to the final harvest of grain is but a few select kernels relative to a vast field of grain, so will the first fruits of the Church be these few individuals who have given all to follow Jesus wherever He goes. The bulk of the Church, the rest of her offspring, will need to undergo purification in the great tribulation to the extent necessary to conform them to the likeness of Jesus. I believe that is why Jesus said, without mentioning option, **"Those who endure to the end will be saved."** It is not because God loves them any less than the first fruits. Their call, however, is to endure the necessary crucible of purification and lay down their lives, if called, in order to overcome Satan. It would seem to be the male child in heaven, the first-fruits harvest of the Church, who speaks forth in Revelation 12:10-11 and identifies those left on earth as "our brethren."

> And I heard a loud voice in heaven saying, "Now the salvation, and the power, and the kingdom of our God and the authority of His Christ have come, for the accuser of **our brethren** has been thrown down, who accuses them before our God day and night. And **they overcame** him because of the blood of the Lamb and because of the word of their testimony, and they did not love their life even to death" (Revelation 12:10-11).

The accuser of the brethren found nothing (no sin) in the first fruits even as he found nothing (no sin) in Jesus, for no lie was found in their mouths and they are blameless. They have been presented to Christ as pure virgins. They have achieved bride status. Those who remain behind are the betrothed who will achieve bride status through purification. Hence, it is not until Revelation 19 that the bride has made herself ready. The tense of the Greek verb used for *overcame* signifies an action not yet completed, but already considered as if completed. The snatching up of the male child at the mid-point of the final seven years would seem to qualify as a "pre-great tribulation" rapture, if these are indeed living saints picked from among the living. For those who would seek to be counted in this group, the qualification is **maturity evidenced by holiness.**

> ... that He might present to Himself the church in all her glory, having no spot or wrinkle or any such thing; but that she should be holy and blameless (Ephesians 5:27).

Who is the Woman?

The book of Revelation is a book of contrasts. Good contrasts evil. The mark of the beast contrasts the mark of God. True prophets contrast false prophets. There is a vision of a woman in Revelation 17 who stands for a great city of evil. Perhaps the identity of the evil woman can provide a clue, by contrast, to the identity of the righteous woman.

If Babylon is the great city represented by the evil woman, the contrasting city represented by the righteous woman would be the holy city of Jerusalem. In Galatians 4:26, we read that the Jerusalem above is indeed portrayed as the mother of the Church. The Lord started me out in understanding who the woman is by speaking a word early one morning in 1997: "Jerusalem above is our mother." He was pointing out existing Scripture.

> For it is written that Abraham had two sons, one by the bondwoman and one by the free woman. But the son by the bondwoman was born according to the flesh, and the son by the free woman through the promise. This is allegorically speaking: for these women are two covenants, one proceeding from Mount Sinai bearing children who are to be slaves; she is Hagar. Now this Hagar is Mount Sinai in Arabia, and corresponds to the present Jerusalem, for she is in slavery with her children. **But the Jerusalem above is free; she is our mother.** For it is written, **"REJOICE, BARREN WOMAN WHO DOES NOT BEAR; BREAK FORTH AND SHOUT, YOU WHO ARE NOT IN LABOR; FOR MORE ARE THE CHILDREN OF THE DESOLATE THAN OF THE ONE WHO HAS A HUSBAND."** And you brethren, like Isaac, are children of promise (Galatians 4:22-28).

> Listen to me, you who pursue righteousness, who seek the LORD: look to the rock from which you were hewn, and to the quarry from which you were dug. Look to Abraham your father, and to **Sarah who gave birth to you in pain** . . . (Isaiah 51:1-2).

> That is, it is not the children of the flesh who are **children of God,** but the **children of the promise** are regarded as descendants. For this is a word of promise; "AT THIS TIME I WILL COME, AND SARAH SHALL HAVE A SON" (Romans 9:8-9).

Sarah stands for the free woman, the Jerusalem above, and her children are the children of God for which all creation awaits. Although Jerusalem above is described as barren and desolate, she is an allegorical representation of the flesh-and-blood, free-and-promised line of Sarah on earth who gives birth to her children in pain out of a physical womb. Jerusalem above represents our spiritual mother while Sarah represents our physical mother. It is God Who transforms the natural into the spiritual, even as He will transform our physical bodies into heavenly bodies.

> And I will put enmity between you and the woman, and between your seed and her seed; he shall bruise you on the head, and you shall bruise him on the heel. To the woman He said, "I will greatly multiply your pain in childbirth, in pain you shall bring forth children . . . " (Genesis 3:15-16).

> But women ["she," margin notes] will be saved ["restored," margin notes] through childbearing — if they continue in faith, love and holiness with propriety (1 Timothy 2:15 NIV).

The Genesis prophecy is clearly in view in the vision of the heavenly woman of Revelation 12. She is a picture of the physical line of Sarah rather than the spiritual Jerusalem above who neither labors nor gives birth. Children are represented in the Bible by a crown, and the crown of twelve stars on her head must represent the twelve sons of Israel and perhaps the twelve foundational apostles of the Church as well. She is still under the Genesis curse and has not yet broken free and been restored. The picture is of a woman struggling in the pains of childbirth to give birth to a portion of the Church at the end of the age, and in the process will be saved and restored. Who, through the process of giving birth, will be restored? Is there a specific people group at the end of the age who flees into the wilderness to be protected from Satan for three and one-half years and is restored through the process of giving birth to a portion of the Church? Who is she, sealed for redemption, yet identified separately from the Church?

God will Never Forget Israel, but have Her Gentile Children?

> Thus says the LORD, who gives the sun for light by day, and the fixed order of the moon and the stars for

> light by night, who stirs up the sea so that its waves roar; the LORD of hosts is His name: **"If** this fixed order departs from before Me," declares the LORD, **"Then** the offspring of Israel also shall cease from being a nation before Me forever." Thus says the LORD, **"If** the heavens above can be measured, and the foundations of the earth searched out below, **then** I will also cast off all the offspring of Israel for all that they have done," declares the LORD (Jeremiah 31:35-37).

We, in understatement to the point of humor, haven't yet measured the heavens above or searched out the depths of the earth, and consequently God has not cast off Israel. Scripture portrays Israel as the wife of God, purposed to bring forth the children of God, even though she is adulterous and unfaithful. She is initially rejected, but will later be accepted and restored.

> Behold, the tempest of the LORD! Wrath has gone forth, a sweeping tempest; it will burst on the head of the wicked. The fierce anger of the LORD will not turn back, until He has performed, and until He has accomplished the intent of His heart; **in the latter days you will understand this.** "At that time," declares the LORD, "I will be the God of all the families of Israel, and they shall be my people." Thus says the LORD, **"The people who survived the sword found grace in the wilderness — Israel, when it went to find its rest"** (Jeremiah 30:23-31:2).

> "Therefore, behold, I will allure her, bring her into the wilderness, and speak kindly to her. Then I will give her her vineyards from there, and the valley of Achor as a door of hope. And she will sing there as in the days of her youth, as in the day when she came up from the land of Egypt. And it will come about in that day," declares the LORD, "That you will call Me Ishi [i.e., my husband] and will no longer call Me Baali [i.e., my master]" (Hosea 2:14-16).

> Then the LORD said to me, "Go again, love a woman who is loved by her husband, yet an adulteress, even as the LORD loves the sons of Israel . . . Afterward the sons of Israel will return and seek the LORD their God and David their king; and they will come trembling to the

LORD and to His goodness in the last days" (Hosea 3:1, 5).

"For the LORD has called you, like a wife forsaken and grieved in spirit, even like a wife of one's youth when she is rejected," says your God. "For a brief moment I forsook you, but with great compassion I will gather you. In an outburst of anger I hid My face from you for a moment; but with everlasting lovingkindness I will have compassion on you," says the LORD your Redeemer (Isaiah 54:6-8).

. . . and I shall bring you into the wilderness of the peoples, and there I shall enter into judgment with you face to face . . . And I shall make you pass under the rod, and I shall bring you into the bond of the covenant (Ezekiel 20:35, 37).

"Behold, the eyes of the Lord GOD are on the sinful kingdom, and I will destroy it from the face of the earth; nevertheless, I will not totally destroy the house of Jacob," declares the LORD. "For behold, I am commanding, and I will shake the house of Israel among all nations as grain is shaken in a sieve, but not a kernel will fall to the ground. All the sinners of My people will die by the sword, those who say, 'The calamity will not overtake or confront us.' In that day I will raise up the fallen booth of David, and wall up its breaches; I will also raise up its ruins, and rebuild it as in the days of old; that they may possess the remnant of Edom and all the nations who are called by My name," declares the LORD who does this (Amos 9:8-12).

I will go away and return to My place until they acknowledge their guilt and seek My face; **in their affliction they will earnestly seek Me.** Come, let us return to the LORD, for He has torn us, but He will heal us; He has wounded us, but He will bandage us. He will revive us after two days; He will raise us up on the third day that we may live before Him (Hosea 5:15-6:2).

Now why do you cry out loudly? Is there no king among you, or has your counselor perished, that agony has gripped you like a woman in childbirth? Writhe and labor to give birth, Daughter of Zion, like a woman in childbirth . . . **Therefore, He will give them up until** the time when she who is in labor has borne a child. Then the remainder of His brethren will return to the sons of Israel (Micah 4:9-10, 5:3).

Although the book of Revelation is written specifically to the Church, the Old Testament is pregnant with prophetic promises to literal Israel which have yet to be fulfilled. God has said that He will never forget His chosen people Israel, yet a largely Gentile Church often does. Paul emphatically lays out the primacy of the Jewishness of the root from which the Gentile branches receive their life-giving sap in Romans Chapter 11. It is because the natural branches have been broken off that the Gentile branches can be grafted in and receive the life that a Jewish Jesus came to offer.

Gentiles are not to be arrogant toward Israel because it is to Israel that Gentiles owe the privilege of coming into attachment to the olive tree from the holy root.

And if the first piece of dough be holy, the lump is also; and if the root be holy, the branches are too. But if some of the branches were broken off, and you, being a wild olive, were grafted in among them and became partaker with them of the rich root of the olive tree, do not be arrogant toward the branches; but if you are arrogant, remember that it is not you who supports the root, but the root supports you (Romans 11:16-18).

For if you were cut off from what is by nature a wild olive tree, and were grafted contrary to nature into a cultivated olive tree, how much more shall these who are the natural branches be grafted into their own olive tree? For I do not want you, brethren, to be uninformed of this mystery, lest you be wise in your own estimation, **that a partial hardening has happened to Israel until the fulness of the Gentiles has come in; and thus all Israel will be saved; just as it is written, "The Deliverer will come from Zion, He will remove ungodliness from Jacob.** And this is My covenant with them, when I take away their sins." From the standpoint of the gospel they are enemies for your sake, but from the standpoint of God's choice they are beloved for the sake of the fathers; for the gifts and the calling of God are irrevocable. For

> just as you once were disobedient to God, but now have been shown mercy **because** of their disobedience, so these also now have been disobedient, in order that because of the mercy shown to you they also may now be shown mercy. For God has shut up all in disobedience that He might show mercy to all. Oh, the depth of the riches both of the wisdom and knowledge of God! How unsearchable are His judgments and unfathomable His ways (Romans 11:24-33)!

Our end-times Church doctrine is often influenced by *replacement theology*, wherein the Church is assumed to replace in spiritual context that which the Bible says is literally applicable to the nation of Israel. References to Zion are assumed to no longer apply to physical Israel, but rather to the Church. Assuredly many of the promises referring to Zion are applicable to the Church, but it is incorrect to assume that the promises no longer apply to Israel because the Church has replaced Israel in the scheme of things. We must remember that there is a heavenly Mt. Zion which represents the one-new-man company of redeemed Jew and Gentile, and there is an earthly Mt. Zion which represents the literal nation of Israel. The earthly Mt. Zion will retain significance throughout the entire one-thousand year reign of Jesus Christ on earth. God has not given up on Israel, and the Bible indicates that the fulfillment of God's restorative promises to Israel have been merely put on hold until the fullness of the Gentiles comes in.

As a consequence of this confusion, Church doctrine concerning the end-times can have the key players mixed up. Israel is often confused for the Church, and vice versa. Israel is placed in view in the warnings of Matthew 24 (which are clearly addressed to Jesus' disciples), and the Church is placed in view in the image of the heavenly woman in Revelation Chapter 12, when it is clearly her offspring who are described as the Church. Israel is a key player in the book of Revelation, but she is behind the scenes struggling in birth pains.

I believe the woman in view in this heavenly vision stands for those of a literal, physical Israel who have been supernaturally blinded for the sake of the Gentiles. This is a group distinct from Messianic Jews. Messianic Jews would be included as part of the Church, either the male child or the offspring of the woman. Paul makes a clear distinction in Romans Chapter 11 between the saved remnant of Israel and those who are hardened and stumble. It is this special group who are hardened and stumble, for the sake of the Gentiles, who are restored at the end of the age when their blindness is removed. When the fullness of the Gentiles has come in, their spiritual vision will be restored by God, and they will be grafted back into the holy olive tree. All of Romans Chapter 11 deals with this point. There must be a special group of Israel, sheltered and protected through the time of Jacob's trouble, so that Scripture can be fulfilled concerning the restoration of that nation which only comes **at the very end** of the age. And these are clearly distinct from that remnant spoken of at the beginning of Romans Chapter 11. These are a part of "all Israel" who will be saved.

Is any portion of the Church included in the woman? After all, Scripture says that all creation is groaning in birth pains. Certainly this heavenly vision is a vision that can apply to all of creation since the fall. Regardless of how widely symbolic the woman is, and how clearly the symbolism of the male child describes Jesus, we are nevertheless constrained to narrow the vision down so that it applies specifically to a group or groups of flesh and blood people alive on the earth during the last three and one-half years of the age. The definition of the Church as those who keep the commandments of God and have faith in Jesus Christ would reserve any living Jew or Gentile who falls into this category as not the woman, but either the male child or the rest of her offspring. The woman would seem to be reserved to those who are specifically not yet Christians, but yet are of the line of Sarah sealed for eventual redemption. I believe the heavenly woman, in the context of the numerous references to Israel struggling in birth pains to give birth to the children of God, is best interpreted as a portrayal of this blinded — but nevertheless sealed for redemption — portion of natural Israel. In a sense, she is the Church — she is just not the Church yet. She is held back from being regenerated until the fullness of the Gentiles has come in.

Mixing these key players can result in loss of vision for the Church's role in the end-times scenario. The woman is specifically protected from Satan and physically preserved until the end of the age, whereas the "rest of her offspring" are warred against by Satan. Their spiritual calling, as we have seen, is to defeat Satan in part by allowing themselves to be physically overcome. This is a crucial distinction which involves the very heart of God's plan for His Church and for Israel.

It is the destiny of this chosen remnant of Israel to be supernaturally protected until the end of the age at which time they will be converted and grafted back in. It is the destiny of the Church to lay down her life as redemptive seed for that conversion and bring this remnant of Israel to jealousy by this witness of these who must have been with Jesus in order to demonstrate this greatest of love for their brethren. Considering the strained history of Jewish-Christian relations for the last two millennia, possibly nothing less than a demonstration of this greatest love possible between brethren will heal that rift. When a largely Gentile Church lives and loves and dies like Jesus did for her Jewish brethren, her Jewish brethren will sit up and take notice.

We were Pregnant, We Writhed in Labor, We gave Birth

> As the pregnant woman approaches the time to give birth, she writhes and cries out in her labor pains, thus were we before Thee, O LORD. We were pregnant, we writhed in labor, we gave birth, as it were, only to wind. We could not accomplish deliverance for the earth nor were inhabitants of the world born (Isaiah 26:17-18).

This is not the Church speaking. These are the words of Zion agonizing in the contractions of childbirth until the purposes of God are brought forth. **"The Deliverer will come from Zion, He will remove ungodliness from Jacob"** is spoken by Paul in Romans 11 in direct contrast to the

Gentile Church he is addressing. This is the woman of Revelation 12 in the pains of the birthing process — Zion on earth laboring in pain to give birth to her children.

The ultimate purposes for which God created the nation of Israel will not be thwarted. **His** covenants with that nation have not been revoked and will never be revoked. It is through Israel that God **will** bless all nations.

> Then God said to Abraham, "As for Sarai your wife, you shall not call her name Sarai, but Sarah shall be her name. And I will bless her, and indeed I will give you a son by her. Then I will bless her, and she shall be a **mother of nations;** kings of peoples shall come from her" (Genesis 17:15-16).

> And the LORD said, "Shall I hide from Abraham what I am about to do, since Abraham will surely become a great and mighty nation, and in him all the nations of the earth will be blessed?" (Genesis 18:17-18).

> . . . for the gifts and the calling of God are irrevocable (Romans 11:29).

> Now if their transgression be riches for the world and their failure be riches for the Gentiles, how much more will their fulfillment be (Romans 11:12)!

Deliverance for the earth and giving birth to inhabitants of the world was their original calling and purpose. Although in the natural and in their own eyes they failed, the purposes of God are not thwarted by mere human shortcoming.

> The children of whom you were bereaved will yet say in your ears, "The place is too cramped for me; make room for me that I may live here." Then you will say in your heart, "Who has begotten these for me, since I have been bereaved of my children, and am barren, an exile and a wanderer? And who has reared these? Behold, I was left alone; from where did these come?" (Isaiah 49:20-21).

"Shout for joy, O barren one, you who have borne no child; break forth into joyful shouting and cry aloud, you who have not travailed; for the sons of the desolate one will be more numerous than the sons of the married woman," says the LORD . . . O afflicted one, storm-tossed, and not comforted, behold I will set your stones in antimony, and your foundations I will lay in sapphires. Moreover, I will make your battlements of rubies, and your gates of crystal, and your entire wall of precious stones. And all your sons will be taught of the LORD; and the well-being of your sons will be great (Isaiah 54:1, 11-13).

"Before she travailed, she brought forth; before her pain came, she gave birth to a **boy.** Who has heard such a thing? Who has seen such things? Can a **land** be born in one day? Can a **nation** be brought forth all at once? As soon as Zion travailed, she also brought forth her **sons.** Shall I bring to the point of birth, and not give delivery?" says the LORD. "Or shall I who gives delivery shut the womb?" says your God (Isaiah 66:7-9).

Nations of the earth **will yet be** considered sons of Israel. This was God's original plan and is still in effect. However, Israel has suffered, is suffering, and must continue to suffer the agony of that birthing until the birthing process is complete.

I looked on the earth, and behold, it was formless and void; and to the heavens, and they had no light. I looked on the mountains, and behold, they were quaking, and all the hills moved to and fro . . . For I heard a cry as of a **woman in labor,** the anguish as of one giving birth to her first child, the cry of the **daughter of Zion** gasping for breath, stretching out her hands, saying, "Ah, woe is me, for I faint before murderers" (Jeremiah 4:23-24, 31).

Now these are the words which the LORD spoke concerning Israel and concerning Judah, "For thus says the LORD, 'I have heard a sound of terror, of dread, and there is no peace. Ask now, and see, if a male can give birth. Why do I see **every man with his hands on his loins, as a woman in childbirth?** And why have all faces turned pale? Alas! for **that day** is great, there is none like it; and it is the time of **Jacob's distress,** but he will be saved from it'" (Jeremiah 30:4-7).

> Now why do you cry out loudly? Is there no king among you, or has your counselor perished, that agony has gripped you like a woman in childbirth? **Writhe and labor to give birth, Daughter of Zion, like a woman in childbirth** . . . Therefore, He will give them up **until the time when she who is in labor has borne a child.** Then the remainder of His brethren will return to the sons of Israel (Micah 4:9-10, 5:3).

The essence of the mystery of Israel and the Church is contained in these Scriptures, which most clearly portray Israel in the form of Zion (or the Daughter of Zion) as the woman of Revelation 12 on earth in the agony of childbirth. This model represents the constraints in which natural chosen Israel has been placed until the fullness of the Gentiles has come in, at which time God will restore this remnant of Israel to the degree of the original promises. She is a special, set-aside remnant of the elect called to a specific purpose — to birth the Gentile Church. This is not about two Churches. This is about a one-new-man company Church under construction (see Ephesians 2:13-22).

Children of the Kingdom, which Israel has not physically birthed, will be attributed to her as her spiritual children. Children of Ruth (Gentiles), fathered in spirit by their Kinsman-Redeemer, will be considered the spiritual children of Naomi (Israel). Even as Obed nursed on Naomi's lap, the nations are portrayed as nursing at the bosom of Jerusalem. It is the mystery of Israel's birthing of the Gentile Church that releases Gentile wombs to reciprocate and be fruitful on Israel's behalf.

> Whenever a woman is in travail she has sorrow, because her hour has come; but when she gives birth to the child, she remembers the anguish no more, for joy that a child has been born into the world (John 16:21).

> "Be joyful with Jerusalem and rejoice for her, all you who love her; be exceedingly glad with her, all you who mourn over her, that you may nurse and be satisfied with her comforting breasts, that you may suck and be delighted with her bountiful bosom." For thus says the LORD, "Behold, I extend peace to her like a river, and the glory of the nations like an overflowing stream; and you

shall be nursed, you shall be carried on the hip and fondled on the knees. As one whom his mother comforts, so I will comfort you; and you shall be comforted in Jerusalem" (Isaiah 66:10-13).

The birth pains she has suffered throughout the age have been to a measurable extent for the benefit of the Gentiles.

> For just as you once were disobedient to God, but now have been shown mercy **because** of their disobedience, so these also now have been disobedient, in order that because of the mercy shown to you they also may now be shown mercy . . . Oh, the depth of the riches both of the wisdom and knowledge of God! How unsearchable are His judgments and unfathomable His ways (Romans 11:30-31, 33)!

May God hasten the day when their blindness will be supernaturally removed and they will say, "Blessed is He Who comes in the name of the Lord!"

> O Jerusalem, Jerusalem, who kills the prophets and stones those who are sent to her! How often I wanted to gather your children together, the way a hen gathers her chicks under her wings, and you were unwilling. Behold, your house is being left to you desolate! For I say to you, from now on you shall not see Me until you say, "BLESSED IS HE WHO COMES IN THE NAME OF THE LORD!" (Matthew 23:37-39).

They will be forgiven, born again, Spirit-filled, and regrafted into the one-new-man company. Let us not fail to incorporate these magnificent promises to Zion into our vision and understand that they are yet to be fulfilled in a restored Jerusalem in a restored Israel.

Until . . .

The irrevocable covenant that God made with Abraham was not dependent on the performance of Israel as a nation. Although the covenant was not revoked, their disobedience brought judgment upon them.

> And he said, "Go, and tell this people: 'Keep on listening, but do not perceive; keep on looking, but do not understand.' Render the hearts of this people insensitive, their ears dull, and their eyes dim, lest they see with their eyes, hear with their ears, understand with their hearts, and return and be healed" (Isaiah 6:9-10).

The woman is still trapped under the Genesis curse until . . .

> Then I said, "Lord, how long?" And He answered, "**Until** cities are devastated and without inhabitant, houses are without people, and the land is utterly desolate, the LORD has removed men far away, and the forsaken places are many in the midst of the land. Yet there will be a tenth portion in it, and it will again be subject to burning, like a terebinth or an oak whose stump remains when it is felled. The holy seed is its stump" (Isaiah 6:11-13).

The fullness of the Gentiles will not come in until Jerusalem ceases to be trampled on by the Gentiles. That does not happen until the very end of the age. The outer court is given to the nations, and the holy city is trampled upon until the very end of the last three and one-half years of the age. This should not be entirely spiritualized, for measuring rods mentioned in the Bible are always used to measure physical objects.

> And there was given me a measuring rod like a staff; and someone said, "Rise and measure the temple of God, and the altar, and those who worship in it. And leave out the court which is outside the temple, and do not measure it, for it has been given to the nations; and **they will tread under foot the holy city for forty-two months**" (Revelation 11:1-2).

> . . . and they will fall by the edge of the sword, and will be led captive into all the nations; and Jerusalem will be **trampled under foot by the Gentiles until** the times of the Gentiles be fulfilled (Luke 21:24).

According to these Scriptures, the times of the Gentiles extend to the very end of the last three and one-half years of the age. Jerusalem is currently being trampled upon by the

Gentiles. That didn't stop in 1967. The outer court is currently given over to the Dome of the Rock. At the time of this writing, Jews cannot worship openly on the temple mount, or an international incident will ensue. Israel **must** remain in partial blindness **until** the times of the Gentiles are fulfilled. The outworking of this will be the ever increasing birth pains known as Jacob's distress or Jacob's trouble. Israel will come to realize that she is but a valley of dry bones. She will be brought to the very end of herself. Her refusal and inability to see up until the very end will bring upon her the increasing throes of the birthing process. And this agony must continue until such time as her children are born.

This is a difficult word, but I believe the level of destruction indicated can only lead to the conclusion that the present nation of Israel, except for a remnant, is an *Ishmael* nation. It was founded and perpetuated largely by the efforts of man, even though the supernatural hand of God was involved, not only in her birthing, but in her survival. Because even the birth of *Ishmaels* serves the ultimate purposes of God. The line of the redeemed, however, is through Isaac and not Ishmael. Not all who are descended from Israel are Israel.

> "Behold, the eyes of the Lord GOD are on the sinful kingdom, and I will destroy it from the face of the earth; nevertheless, I will not totally destroy the house of Jacob," declares the LORD (Amos 9:8).

The prophetic Scriptures which detail the destruction of Jerusalem at the very end of the age are too many and too descriptive to allow cataloging that destruction in history past. Israel's judgments are a direct result of their refusal to turn to their God. Since the present nation still refuses to turn to their God and is firmly entrenched in the same activities that led to prior judgments, increasing judgment must come. The original promises to Moses in the form of blessings and curses depend on the heart of the people toward their God and clearly indicate that when the nation perseveres in ignoring their God, God will persevere in increasing His judgments against them **until** they can no longer ignore Him. And this last judgment will be one that is so devastating in magnitude and in the nature of its supernatural reversal and restoration that it is always followed by these words, **"And then they will know that I am God."** In the ashes of yet another future holocaust will be found the remnant seed that God will supernaturally restore. It is the Gentile Church's call not only to stand by their blinded brethren during this time of devastation, but also to lay down their lives when called as redemptive seed in that restoration. The birth of the restored nation will be a supernatural birth that will stagger all of creation. **Then** they will know that **HE** is God. The present nation does not yet know and chooses not to consider it, hence the increasing magnitude of the judgment that must come to get their attention and turn them back to their God.

If she is a sign of physically sealed Israel held in the constraints of childbirth for the benefit of the Gentiles, then we should be able to identify somewhere in Scripture such a group of Israelites specifically protected on earth from the onslaughts of Satan during the last three and one-half years of the age. Such a group matches the initial group of 144,000 bondservants of Revelation 7, selected from twelve tribes of Israel and protected from the demonic assaults of the fifth trumpet judgment. This will be further explored in the next chapter.

The One-new-man Company

> Therefore remember, that formerly you, the Gentiles in the flesh, who are called "Uncircumcision" by the so-called "Circumcision," which is performed in the flesh by human hands — remember that you were at that time separate from Christ, excluded from the commonwealth of Israel, and strangers to the covenants of promise, having no hope and without God in the world. But now in Christ Jesus you who formerly were far off have been brought near by the blood of Christ. For He Himself is our peace, who made both groups into one, and broke down the barrier of the dividing wall, by abolishing in His flesh the enmity, which is the Law of commandments

contained in ordinances, that in Himself He might make the two into **one new man,** thus establishing peace, and might reconcile them both in **one body** to God through the cross, by it having put to death the enmity (Ephesians 2:11-16).

It is **this Church** and no other that Paul identifies in Ephesians 3:10 as the Church that will allow the demonstration of God's wisdom to the rulers and authorities in the heavenly places. Micah 5:3 continues to take on greater clarity.

> Therefore, He will give them up until the time when she who is in labor has borne a child. Then the remainder of His brethren will return to the sons of Israel (Micah 5:3).

What does it mean that the remainder of His brethren will return to the sons of Israel, other than the rest of the woman's offspring in the form of a largely Gentile Church will come into union with God's originally chosen people? It will not be a Church divided or a Church that has replaced Zion. It will be His brethren returning to Zion, and the two will become the one-new-man Church, represented spiritually by the Heavenly Jerusalem located on the Heavenly Mount Zion.

> But you have come to Mount Zion and to the city of the living God, the heavenly Jerusalem, and to myriads of angels, to the general assembly and church of the first-born who are enrolled in heaven, and to God, the Judge of all, and to the spirits of righteous men made perfect, and to Jesus, the mediator of a new covenant, and to the sprinkled blood, which speaks better than the blood of Abel (Hebrews 12:22-24).

The woman of Revelation 12 is not yet the New Jerusalem of Revelation 21. The New Jerusalem will be a one-new-man company of Jew and Gentile comprising all of the redeemed of history, established by God after the millennial reign of Christ on earth from the earthly Mt. Zion in earthly Jerusalem. The woman and her children of Revelation 12 will eventually make up the New Jerusalem, but at the time of the vision, she, along with her children, are components of that future city still in the stages of restoration and development. As of Revelation 12, the bride has not yet made herself ready. As of today, Israel has not yet returned to their God, and the Church is not yet a bride without spot or wrinkle. But praise God, we are in the midst of birth pains ever increasingly designed to make us that way.

"Father, we desperately need Your wisdom and revelation to understand especially these Scriptures. The mystery of Your chosen people Israel and Your Church seem to be the very heart of this heavenly vision. Would You pour out fresh revelation into these areas so that we are armed with proper understanding and vision as we enter the very end of the age. Enlarge our understanding and vision, Father, of these things. Thank You, Father, for allowing Gentiles to be ingrafted as branches of the tree of the Holy Root. Thank You that because of the disobedience of one, another has been given mercy; and that because of the mercy given to another, mercy will be given to the one. Oh Lord, save Your people, the remnant of Israel. As we meditate on these awesome Scriptures, the love for Your chosen people burns in our hearts! May the peace of Jerusalem come forth! May Your Word and Law proceed forth from Jerusalem and may all nations, as sons of Israel, come to that place of blessing to witness the brightness of Your Glory. Come quickly, Lord Jesus. Amen."

THIRTEEN

Who are the 144,000(s)?

And I saw another angel ascending from the rising of the sun, having the seal of the living God; and he cried out with a loud voice to the four angels to whom it was granted to harm the earth and the sea, saying, "Do not harm the earth or the sea or the trees, until we have sealed the bond-servants of our God on their foreheads." And I heard the number of those who were sealed, **one hundred and forty-four thousand sealed from every tribe of the sons of Israel** . . . (Revelation 7:2-4).

And I looked, and behold, the Lamb was standing on Mount Zion, and with Him **one hundred and forty-four thousand, having His name and the name of His Father written on their foreheads.** And I heard a voice from heaven, like the sound of many waters and like the sound of loud thunder, and the voice which I heard was like the sound of harpists playing on their harps. And they sang a new song before the throne and before the four living creatures and the elders; and no one could learn the song except the one hundred and forty-four thousand who had been purchased from the earth. These are the ones who have not been defiled with women, for they have kept themselves chaste. These are the ones who follow the Lamb wherever He goes. These have been purchased from among men as **first fruits** to God and to the Lamb. And no lie was found in their mouth; they are blameless (Revelation 14:1-5).

We should not automatically assume that the first group of 144,000 in Revelation Chapter 7 is the same group presented in Chapter 14. There are significant differences between the two groups, both in their descriptions and the timing of their appearances on the scene. Those of Chapter 7 are selected from every tribe of Israel, while those of Chapter 14 are selected from among men. Those of Chapter 14 are in heaven before the gospel is preached to the whole world and before the trumpet judgments, while those of Chapter 7 are on earth after the preaching of the gospel to the whole world, being sealed to go through the trumpet judgments. Those in Chapter 7 are marked with the seal of God on their foreheads, while those in Chapter 14 are marked with the name of God **and the name of the Lamb** on their foreheads.

The 144,000 of Revelation Chapter 7

The first group of 144,000 in Revelation Chapter 7 from the twelve tribes of Israel is sealed during the time delay between the sixth and seventh seals to protect them from the oncoming wrath of God in the form of the trumpet judgments. They are mentioned at the time of the fifth trumpet as being protected from the demonic hordes. Satan has obviously been released in the trumpet judgments to serve as an instrument of God's wrath. This is a much different function of Satan than was allowed during the great tribulation, where the saints were subject to the limited fury of Satan. Satan was tethered on a restraining leash during the great tribulation, but in the trumpets he is given more rope. Satan's restrained fury, evidenced against the Church during the great tribulation, will pale in comparison to God's wrath allowed in the form of the trumpet judgments. But the Church is not appointed to God's wrath. The Blood of Jesus will protect the Church from God's wrath even as the blood on the doorposts of the Israelites protected them from the plagues that befell Egypt. The similarities between some of the plagues of Egypt and some of the trumpet judgments are obvious.

We, the Church, are sealed with the seal of the Holy Spirit when we are born again. We won't need another seal applied just before the trumpet judgments to protect us from God's wrath.

> For God has not destined us for wrath . . . (1 Thessalonians 5:9).

We are protected and will continue to be protected from God's wrath and from Satan and his demonic hordes, and **not** by being removed from the earth.

> I do not ask Thee to take them out of the world, but to keep [protect, NIV] them from the evil one (John 17:15).

Jesus' prayer **has** been answered. We must remember, however, that being kept and protected from Satan in this context is not the same as being protected from physical death at the hands of Satan, which will be allowed during the great tribulation. Being protected from Satan as used in this context refers to being protected from being spiritually overcome. It has nothing to do with preserving our earthly lives.

> But you will be delivered up even by parents and brothers and relatives and friends, and they will put some of you to death, and you will be hated by all on account of My name. Yet not a hair of your head will perish. By your endurance you will gain your lives (Luke 21:16-19).

Not a hair of our heads will perish, and by our endurance we will gain our lives — even though we may be put to death. This is an eternal perspective, not an earthly one, and one which makes sense only to those who have put their total trust in Jesus Christ and see eternity beyond as more real than this life's transient vapor.

> In Him, you also, after listening to the message of truth, the gospel of your salvation — having also believed, **you were sealed in Him** with the Holy Spirit of promise, who is given as a pledge of our inheritance, with a view to

the redemption of God's own possession, to the praise of His glory (Ephesians 1:13-14).

Now He who establishes us with you in Christ and anointed us is God, who also **sealed us** and gave us the Spirit in our hearts as a pledge (2 Corinthians 1:21-22).

If They were the Church, They would Already be Sealed!

The Scriptures we have just looked at indicate that, by definition, the Church is sealed and protected from God's wrath. Why then does this group of 144,000 from twelve tribes of Israel need special provision between the sixth and seventh seals to protect them from the beginning of wrath which follows the breaking of the seventh seal?

Those who hold to the pre-tribulation rapture position will say that all this indicates that the Church has already been raptured and that these 144,000 are Jewish evangelists left on earth during the last three and one-half years to preach the gospel. But according to pre-trib logic, if they are evangelists believing in Jesus, they would have been raptured with the rest of the Church. And if they are not believers in Jesus, they cannot preach the gospel. There must be another explanation as to who these 144,000 are. *Don't they say that they become Christians after the rapture + then evangelize?*

Since the Church does not need to have things put on hold between the sixth and seventh seals until they are given a special seal to protect them from God's wrath, this must be a special group not yet sealed with the Holy Spirit. Their sealing at this time does not prove prior rapture; it is a special sealing of those not yet covered by the Blood of the Lamb. Who is this unique Jewish group, identified and sealed for protection at this time, apparently not previously sealed with the Holy Spirit, yet referred to as bondservants? I believe the descriptions of the markings on their foreheads, though subtle in difference, may be important.

Matching the 144,000 of Revelation 7 with the Woman of Revelation 12

The conclusions of the last chapter were that a reserved and blinded remnant of Israel must be supernaturally protected during the last three and one-half years of the age in order to fulfill the prophetic role of Zion destined for labor pains until her children are brought forth. These 144,000 of Revelation 7 fit that description. They are reserved for salvation at the end of the age, but not yet covered by the Blood of the Lamb at the time of the trumpet judgments. They will need special provision to survive until the end of the age. They are protected from Satan during the great tribulation as they flee into the wilderness. In addition, they are sealed here for protection from the wrath of God so that they can survive until the fullness of the Gentiles comes in at the end of the age at which time they will be brought into the New Covenant of the Blood of Jesus Christ.

> And out of the smoke came forth locusts upon the earth; and power was given them, as the scorpions of the earth have power. And they were told that they should not hurt the grass of the earth, nor any green thing, nor any tree, **but only the men who do not have the seal of God on their foreheads** (Revelation 9:3-4).

In addition to these 144,000 reserved Israelites who have the seal of God on their foreheads, every living member of the Church of Jesus Christ left on earth is already sealed with the seal of the Holy Spirit. Those marked and protected with the seal of God and the Holy Spirit will directly contrast those sealed with the mark of Satan. Everyone on the planet will wear one seal or the other. There will be no neutral ground. Satan is a counterfeiter, and when he sees the seal of God on the forehead of the male child in the form of the name of God and the name of the Lamb (Revelation 14:1), he will respond with his own counterfeit mark to be placed on the wrist or forehead of his own sons.

The 144,000 of Revelation 14: A Different Group!

I believe that the beginning of Revelation Chapter 14 is a flashback because the preaching of the gospel to the entire world described in Revelation 14:6, which takes place during the last three and one-half years of the age, has to have already taken place by the sixth seal. This has to be true because in order for the great multitude of Revelation 7:9 to have come out of the great tribulation **from every nation and tribe and people and tongue,** they had to have had the gospel preached to them! There must, therefore, be two independent groups of 144,000 in view, as one group would not be identified both in heaven before the great tribulation is over and also on earth being marked so as to be protected from the trumpet judgments which follow that great tribulation.

First Fruits

> You shall count fifty days to the day after the seventh sabbath; then you shall present a new grain offering to the LORD. You shall bring in from your dwelling places **two loaves** of bread for a wave offering, made of two-tenths of an ephah; they shall be of a fine flour, **baked with leaven as first fruits** to the LORD (Leviticus 23:16-17).

> And you shall celebrate the Feast of Weeks, that is, the **first fruits of the wheat harvest**... (Exodus 34:22).

The two loaves of the Feast of Weeks (also known as the Feast of Harvest of the First Fruits) that are baked with leaven (as opposed to the unleavened bread representing Jesus) are commonly considered as representing the Church, composed of redeemed Jew and Gentile. The day of this feast, when the two loaves of bread are brought before the Lord as a grain wave offering of first fruits, is also known as the day of Pentecost.

> And when the day of Pentecost had come, they were all together in one place. And suddenly there came from heaven a noise like a violent, rushing wind, and it filled

the whole house where they were sitting. And there appeared to them tongues as of fire distributing themselves, and they rested on each one of them. And they were all filled with the Holy Spirit and began to speak with other tongues, as the Spirit was giving them utterance . . . but this is what was spoken of through the prophet Joel: "AND IT SHALL BE IN THE LAST DAYS," God says, "THAT I WILL POUR FORTH OF MY SPIRIT UPON **ALL** MANKIND; AND YOUR SONS AND YOUR DAUGHTERS SHALL PROPHESY, AND YOUR YOUNG MEN SHALL SEE VISIONS, AND YOUR OLD MEN SHALL DREAM DREAMS; EVEN UPON MY BONDSLAVES, BOTH MEN AND WOMEN, I WILL IN THOSE DAYS POUR FORTH OF MY SPIRIT and they shall prophesy. AND I WILL GRANT WONDERS IN THE SKY ABOVE, AND SIGNS ON THE EARTH BENEATH, BLOOD, AND FIRE, AND VAPOR OF SMOKE. THE SUN SHALL BE TURNED INTO DARKNESS, AND THE MOON INTO BLOOD, BEFORE THE GREAT AND GLORIOUS DAY OF THE LORD SHALL COME. AND IT SHALL BE, THAT EVERYONE WHO CALLS ON THE NAME OF THE LORD SHALL BE SAVED" (Acts 2:1-4,16-21).

Matching the 144,000 of Revelation 14:1 with the Male Child

As presented in the previous chapter, I believe this second group of 144,000 of Revelation 14:1 is the male child of Revelation 12:5. The offspring of the woman of Revelation 12 are two: the "male child" and the "rest of her offspring." The rest of her offspring are clearly identified as the saints warred against by the dragon (Satan), while the male child is snatched up to heaven out of reach of Satan's grasp. This snatching up is described as taking place at the three and one-half year point (the midpoint) of the final seven years of the age, and it corresponds in timing to Revelation 14:1 where we see the 144,000 in heaven before the gospel is preached to the entire world. This preaching of the gospel to the entire world will be the substance of the last three and one-half years of the age, performed by a Church in the anointing and authority and power described in Revelation 12:10.

They have matured early as first fruits into the likeness of Jesus. There is no need for them to be further tested and refined by the great tribulation, as they are ready to be taken into the house of God. Hence they may correspond to the overcoming saints of the church of Philadelphia who are said to be kept from the hour of testing coming upon the whole earth and who have the Father's name and the name of Jesus on their foreheads. They may also correspond to the overcoming saints of the church of Thyatira who will rule the nations with a rod of iron. All indications are that they are a mixed company of Jew and Gentile.

What is revealed here may indeed be a pre-tribulation rapture, but if so, it is a *pre-great tribulation* rapture of only the select few who will qualify as first fruits. The bulk of the saints will not have ripened sufficiently before the great tribulation to qualify. Satan still has something in them that has to be burned out by the purifying fires of tribulation in order to make them worthy of the Kingdom of God and refine them into the bride company without spot or wrinkle.

All indications are that a great outpouring of the Holy Spirit takes place at this point when the male child in the form of the first fruits is snatched up to heaven and Satan is hurled to earth.

> And I heard a loud voice in heaven, saying, "Now the salvation, and the power, and the kingdom of our God and the authority of His Christ have come, for the accuser of our brethren has been thrown down, who accuses them before our God day and night" (Revelation 12:10).

This power and authority and salvation and evidence of God's Kingdom which comes to earth are descriptive of what happened when the Holy Spirit fell on the day of Pentecost two thousand years ago. It takes place here again at the end of the age, at the timing of the waving of the first fruits before the Lord, i.e., the snatching up of the male child.

The first fruits are speaking from heaven in Revelation 12:11 prophesying the victory of **their brethren** left on earth who will overcome Satan by the Blood of the Lamb, the word of their testimony, and by loving not their lives unto death.

Micah 5:3

> Therefore, He will give them up until the time when she who is in labor has borne a child. Then the remainder of **His brethren** will return to the sons of Israel (Micah 5:3).

The makeup of the one-new-man first-fruits company of Jew and Gentile that forms the male child will establish the standard for those remaining on the earth. It will be a call to a primarily Gentile Church left on earth to establish the proper understanding and relationship to God's chosen people of irrevocable covenant. There is definitely a returning and a rejoining that takes place during this period of time **after** the birth of the male child. The Church that will demonstrate the wisdom of God to the rulers and authorities in the heavenly places during the last three and one-half years of the age can only be a one-new-man Church comprised of redeemed Jew and Gentile.

FOURTEEN

Who is the Bride?

And a voice came from the throne, saying, "Give praise to our God, **all you His bond-servants, you who fear Him, the small and the great.**" And I heard, as it were, the voice of a great multitude and as the sound of many waters and as the sound of mighty peals of thunder, saying, "Hallelujah! For the Lord our God, the Almighty, reigns. Let us rejoice and be glad and give the glory to Him, for the marriage of the Lamb has come and **His bride has made herself ready.**" And it was given to her to clothe herself in fine linen, bright and clean; for the fine linen is the righteous acts of the saints. And he said to me, "Write, 'Blessed are those who are invited to the marriage supper of the Lamb.'" And he said to me, "These are the true words of God" (Revelation 19:5-9).

By this time in the course of events, the great tribulation is over, the harvest of the living and the dead in Christ has taken place, the harlot of Babylon has been destroyed, and the wrath of God has been fully poured out on the beast and his kingdom. Only after all of these things have taken place has the bride made herself ready. Who is she and why did it take so long for her to get dressed? Apparently her wedding garments, which stand for the righteous acts of the saints, are not finished until all of these events are completed.

The bride cannot be reserved to just those alive at the end of the age, for Jesus came as the bridegroom two thousand years ago, and it was the church members at Corinth that Paul was eager to present as spiritual virgins to Christ the husband (2 Corinthians 11:2). However, Scripture indicates that the bride company will not be ready until the very end of the age, not only in total numbers but also in maturity. He's coming back for a bride without spot or wrinkle.

There are a number of clues to the identity of the bride. She is not ready until the great tribulation is over. She is dressed in white garments which are the righteous acts of the saints. She will be the people of a heavenly city whose gates stand for the twelve tribes of Israel and whose foundation stones stand for the twelve apostles (Revelation 21:12-14). I believe this indicates that the saints of Old Testament Israel are included in the bride company. The bride would then include every Blood-redeemed Jew and Gentile from all of history, in addition to those last-generation saints of Revelation who have just emerged victorious from great tribulation. These saints are the last portion of the bride company for which completion of the bride awaits. Following the roll-call of the Old Testament *hall of faith* saints of Hebrews 11, the writer of Hebrews reveals:

> And all these, having gained approval through their faith, did not receive what was promised, because God had provided something better for us, so that apart from us they should not be made perfect. Therefore, since we have so great a cloud of witnesses surrounding us, let us also lay aside every encumbrance, and the sin which so easily entangles us, and let us run with endurance the race that is set before us (Hebrews 11:39-12:1).

The staggering indication of Scripture is that the perfection of the Old Testament saints depends on the race run by the Church, and the outcome of that race will be decided by the last leg of the race run at the very end of this age. If the Church at the end of the age drops the baton, all of creation will lose. No wonder Satan is working overtime to trip up this final generation of the Church and lead them into deception. But we already know that the Church will be victorious. That's settled. **Jesus is King.** God will successfully demonstrate His wisdom through the Church to the rulers and authorities in the heavenly places. The Church will rule and reign on earth with Jesus for one-thousand years. The question for each of us is, will we as individuals be among those who endure and are victorious, or will we be among those who fall away?

The bride is not completed until after the pouring out of the sixth bowl, for it is at the sixth bowl in Revelation 16:15 that the parenthetical statement of Jesus is heard:

> (Behold, I am coming like a thief. Blessed is the one who stays awake and keeps his garments, lest he walk about naked and men see his shame.)

This speaks of the need to keep our spiritual garments of righteousness tightly wrapped around us right up until the very end. If our love should grow cold, as Jesus said the love of most would, then the righteous acts that make up our wedding garments will not be forthcoming, and we will stand naked and ashamed before the King.

We have considered that this is the remnant to make up the final component of the Bride of Christ, the gleanings of the harvest saved at the last minute by fearing God and giving Him glory. The great multitude of the bride company rejoicing before the throne is made up of not just bondservants and saints, but also those who fear God, the small and the great. This is in keeping with the observation that God's judgments in the form of the trumpets, and even the bowls, are redemptive and allow the provision for salvation up until the very last bowl.

The parable that describes this multitude would be that of the workers who were paid the same regardless of the hour when they were hired. There will be a distribution of rewards in heaven, but the bride company does not seem reserved for a select few. The bride seems to consist of the elect from all of history redeemed by the Blood of the Lamb. However, for purposes of restoring the vision of the Church, we can be less concerned about who she is in her historical fullness than who she is in **character**. For it is her character that we, who aspire to be the Bride of Christ, must develop and exhibit. The purifying crucible of the great tribulation will have burned away the last vestige of impurity from those saints of the last generation who make their robes white by washing with the Blood of the Lamb.

> ... that He might present to Himself the church in all her glory, having no spot or wrinkle or any such thing; but that she should be holy and blameless (Ephesians 5:27).

The great tribulation must therefore be embraced as the necessary fires of purification which transform the last-generation Church into this required degree of perfection. Those who have sought and found the grace to develop as first fruits will not need this time of testing. But for the rest of the Church, these times must be embraced as times designed specifically to conform her into the likeness of Jesus and to qualify her as His bride. Should this cost our physical lives, praise God Who gives only what is needed to transform us into a bride without spot or wrinkle.

The last three and one-half years of this age will be the capstone of the Church age and the time for which the finest wine and greater glory of the latter house have been reserved. This is the Church at the very end of the age through which God will complete the demonstration of His wisdom to the rulers and authorities in the heavenly places. It is upon this last generation of saints that God will pour out the fullness of His power and anointing. The stature which these saints at the very end of the age will attain serves as prerequisite for the perfection of the entire body of the elect. We need to carefully consider the characteristics of the bride, particularly the purity of her wedding garments. We need to understand the degree of purity to which we are called. We must incorporate these requirements into our vision. We must cast off the sin which so easily besets us and run this race with endurance.

A Bride without Spot, Wrinkle, or Blemish

Jude 23 indicates that flesh can pollute an otherwise clean garment. The impurities which must be washed away in order to achieve bride status are then not just the overt sins we commonly associate with sin, but also the pollution of flesh (self), i.e., **our own fleshly, soulish life in the form of antichrist motive, will, desires, preferences, agendas, efforts, etc.** Holy and blameless will apply only to those who have given **all** to follow Jesus. The final bride company will consist of those who have been purified to this degree. Perhaps the great tribulation will be more concerned with burning away these impurities rather than the more obvious sins we normally associate as *sin*. We are called to follow the Lamb **wherever** He goes. To the extent that we do not, it is sin which must be purged. To the extent that we have allowed our garments to remain spotted, we have done away with the cross and not embraced it to the extent required.

> For the flesh sets its desire against the Spirit, and the Spirit against the flesh; for these are in opposition to one another, so that you **may not** do the things that you please (Galatians 5:17).

> For I am jealous for you with a godly jealousy; for I betrothed you to one husband, that to Christ I might present you as a pure virgin (2 Corinthians 11:2).

The Work of the Lord, or Our Work?

It is not sufficient to do the *work of the Lord* in our time and season, for then it is not the work of the Lord, but our work. It is but **wood, hay, and stubble** which will not survive the testing fires. We will be known by our fruits. But deeds done in our own time and season and energy, even in the name of Jesus, will not qualify as good fruit.

> So then, you will know them by their fruits. Not everyone who says to Me, "Lord, Lord," will enter the kingdom of heaven; but he who does the will of My Father who is in heaven. Many will say to Me on that

day, "Lord, Lord, did we not prophesy in Your name, and in Your name cast out demons, and in Your name perform many miracles?" And then I will declare to them, "I never knew you; DEPART FROM ME, YOU WHO PRACTICE LAWLESSNESS" (Matthew 7:20-23).

These are Kingdom-like works that Jesus is calling lawlessness! Jesus only did what He saw the Father doing. The above prophecies and miracles turned out to be not what the Father was doing, and those who performed them were judged as practicing lawlessness. **We must come to the point where we despise doing anything, even works in His name, in our own timing.**

The church in Ephesus seemed to have everything going for it. They were commended on their deeds, their toil, their perseverance, their intolerance of evil, their discernment of false apostles, and their zeal in enduring and not growing weary amidst all of this. How many of us qualify for even this commendation? And yet Jesus singled out their great loss of having left their first love and called them to repent, or their lampstand would be removed.

This **must** be a wake-up call to establish the proper priorities. **Blessed is the one who stays awake and keeps his garments.** The work in the kitchen must never supersede being at Jesus' feet. For it is only at Jesus' feet that we will come to know Him and be known by Him. Only then will we be in position to see what He is doing, and only then will we be able to carry out those perfect works chosen for us to do, in His strength, before time began. These are the only works that will pass the test of fire. Mindless performance of *good* things is disobedience. The fruit from the tree of good and evil is poisonous, be it good or evil. Only fruit from the tree of life sustains.

Several years ago, the Lord clearly led me to visit a hospital one Sunday with a church home group to pray for a badly burned young boy who was brain dead and existing only on life support. The Lord miraculously healed him. I got in the habit after that of routinely visiting hospitals and praying for the sick. I thought it was a good thing to do and that the Lord was behind it all. But visits to other patients seemed strangely dry and unanointed. One day, as I was riding to a hospital, an old vintage Cadillac pulled slowly alongside, and the license plate read "CCIM-VK." I am VK, so that part of the message I understood. About thirty minutes later, the meaning of "CCIM" came to me: **"Seek Him."** I sensed that the Lord was teaching me the difference between my works in my time and His works in His time. The priority was to seek first the Kingdom of God and His righteousness, and from that all things would properly flow both in content and timing.

Seeking Him must always be our priority. Only out of seeking Him will we know His perfect work for us at any given time. Perhaps His perfect work for us today is to sit and be silent before Him. I was being disobedient as I arbitrarily visited hospitals thinking that I was doing the will of God. It was not His choice in His timing. We must be led by the Spirit of God. Only those who are led by the Spirit are children of God. The rest are practicing lawlessness. Hence those who visit hospitals thinking they are doing the will of God, but are not acting based on the hearing of His voice, are in danger of having their deeds called deeds of lawlessness. Can we receive this? Remember, Scripture **does say** that some of those who do miracles in His name **will have their deeds judged as evil.** We will always receive the praises of men when we visit nursing homes and hospitals and prisons, but we may not always receive the praise of our Lord. What were our motives for the visit? Was it obedience to His call or was it something that we thought we should be doing or wanted to do based on a self-serving motive or a spirit of man-pleasing? It may have been a good thing, but was it His thing? The good fruit of the tree of death is not only as deadly as the evil fruit, but it is much more deceptive. **We must not minister primarily based on the needs around us, but on direct leading of the Lord.**

The bride company has been stripped of all such impurity. They have learned to follow the Lamb wherever He goes, as they have learned to recognize His voice amidst deafening chaos and confusion. They have consented to let

God do that work in them which results in them living for Him rather than for themselves.

I started out in my Christian walk motivated and zealous — in the flesh. After about two years of this, the Lord stopped me dead in my tracks and sat me down and had me open Charles Finney's *Letter to New Christians*. The Holy Spirit fell on me like a hot, heavy blanket, and I found myself weeping while wrapped in His arms of love as He proceeded to tell me that I had betrayed Jesus even as Judas had betrayed Him with a kiss. "What difference would it make to the Kingdom if there were millions like you?" He asked. It was a scathing rebuke. But it was given with His perfect love that casts out all fear. I felt privileged to be a son so disciplined. The Holy Spirit prompted me to consider that Finney's letter was written on February 13, 1839. I was reading it on December 13, 1992. That works out to 153 years and ten months later, 153 being the number of fish captured in the net of John 21.

I believe this has something to do with becoming fishers of men. Unless Jesus is living in us and through us, we cannot become effective fishers of men, and we betray Him by speaking of Him and doing for Him. We've got to get this through our heads. The priority in our Christian walk is to **seek Him!** We must wait in our Jerusalems! We must not go until we are filled with power from on high. Many teach that we are already told to go. But when we get to the mission field, be it overseas or next door, and we find ourselves powerless and unanointed, then something has been missed. Perhaps we have missed considering that the great commission is a two-part directive: **wait** in Jerusalem until you receive power from on high, and **then** go and make disciples of all nations. I have read too many testimonies of saints who were on the mission field for twenty years before they realized that Jesus is **all,** and that they needed to be filled with Him and not themselves. And it matches what the Lord seems to be telling me in my own experience. We have nothing to offer the nations or our next door neighbors until we are overflowing with living water.

Furthermore, after the disciples were told to go into the world and make fellow disciples of all nations, Paul was prevented by the Holy Spirit from preaching the gospel in Asia. Does that violate our theology? Do we think we have the commission to do things in our time and season? Quite obviously we do not. We must learn to hear His voice and to be led by it. And whether we have to wait in prayer and fasting in Jerusalems at home or on the mission field, we must wait until we are filled with the Holy Spirit and overflowing with living water or we are betraying Him of Whom we speak.

There is truth in the analogy that a ship without movement cannot be steered. Stagnation is not an option. But we must be **LED** by the Holy Spirit. There is a balance here that must be worked out with fear and trembling, and it can only be worked out by listening at the feet of Jesus.

"Father, create a work in us which strips us of that self which always places our priorities first and sees even the things of Christianity as things to be grasped to be used for selfish motives and agendas. Quiet the roar of self within us, Father, that keeps us from hearing and wanting to hear Your still small voice. Father, we offer ourselves as living sacrifices so that You may do this work in us. Father, forgive our many attempts to casually retake what we may have once intently devoted to You. Do a work in us, Father, which will stand the test of the fires that are coming upon the earth."

A Deeper Death

The death of self is that living sacrifice that we are all called to make. The death of self is the cross that must be picked up daily in order to follow Jesus. This is a deeper and a more difficult death to live out than the martyr's death.

Self can so easily masquerade as the good, when in fact it is something that needs to be put to death. The Scriptures have pointed out how futile all things good are and how really only one thing is necessary. We should not be seeking to do good deeds, but only those deeds that Jesus prescribes, for those will be the deeds that follow after us. How much of our walk is still tarnished by the misconception that our deeds somehow add something to our worthiness, when Scripture clearly says that our deeds will follow us, not precede us, into the Kingdom? The priority then becomes to "CCIM" until we hear His voice, and then obey it. The self will consciously or unconsciously seek to block that voice, for the Spirit and the flesh are at war. The clamor of self preference will block out the still small voice until God allows us to become so desperate that we gladly agree to lay all of self at the foot of the cross. And until we do, God will take us through painful processes that ever increasingly make us realize He and He alone is to be the end of all our seeking and the antidote for our distress.

The Absence of the Cross

The absence of the cross permeates more of our *Christian* walk than we realize. Why is it that our shadows do not heal and our words are not God's words? We read in the Bible that Jesus never did anything that He did not see the Father doing, and yet we are cursed with theologies that teach that God doesn't speak today. How are we going to move in those perfect works that God has chosen for us unless we hear His voice? Jesus did good works but He only did those good works He saw the Father doing. We can't read about what Jesus did and then go out and do those things unless we have waited in our Jerusalems until the Father has told us which ones to do and when to do them. We are so full of ourselves and our own teachings and motives and agendas that we find no need to hear the voice of God telling us how and when to move. Consequently, we are powerless. We do not heal the sick and raise the dead and feed the multitudes from a few fish and loaves. **We have many words, but we have little power.** It is perhaps the weakness of the conversions in the face of such luke-warm teachings that will result in the love of most growing cold and many falling away when the times of testing come.

They have Done Away with the Cross

Several years ago I attended a large Christian gathering in Honolulu. I thought it would be a good thing to do. I attended all of the preliminary meetings designed to equip us to be ushers and counselors. Armed with pledge cards and evangelistic zeal, we stormed the arena floor following the altar call eager to sweep many into the Kingdom.

In my case, no one I approached wanted prayer or consultation. I approached several groups who were okay as they were, thanks anyway. Finally I forced myself into a group and prayed a lifeless prayer that fell to the ground like sawdust. Wearied and discouraged, I made my way back up to my seat in the stands and collapsed into it and sat there like a lump wondering what had just happened.

I could see that down on the floor others were involved in getting cards signed and doing the things that we were trained to do. But a heaviness was on me that barely allowed me to stand through the closing music, even though there was plenty of cheering and enthusiasm and hand waving.

On the way home I expressed to my friends that I knew that God had spoken, but I wasn't clear on what He had said. No one in my group had sensed what I had sensed. My only thought was that I had miserably failed in some required area.

I could not attend the following day. I was drained of all energy and enthusiasm. As I rolled over in bed following my car pool wake-up call, my eyes focused on David Wilkerson's latest newsletter. I had glanced at it the night before after coming home from the meeting, but at that time it was just words. But this morning was different. The title read, *They Have Done Away With the Cross.* Instantly the flush of the Holy Spirit told me that God had spoken. How could it be that they had done away with the cross? They had the best music, the best speakers, seemingly the right words about relationship — what was missing? Maybe it was I who had done away with the cross?

Was there something critical I had missed? I tried feeling out the subject with a few of my friends, but their response was not enthusiastic. What did it mean to "do away with the cross?" I have spent almost two years trying to figure out what He meant. Slowly and steadily over the course of those two years God showed me that we had all done away with the cross that night.

I believe we have been blinded with regard to the deeper depths of repentance and cleansing that the cross requires. That deeper depth is the death and burial of self. Until that death is apprehended by faith, the resurrection to follow in His power and authority can never be realized. Hence, we remain powerless and wretched and miserable and poor and blind and naked, unaware and deceived as to our true state. The world will never be changed by such as these. We betray rather than portray Christ when we speak of Him.

May God give us mercy to comprehend our true stature — that there is nothing good in us, that there is not one of us that does good, and that our place of worship needs to be prostrate at the foot of the cross in acknowledgment of our true state. The flesh can never be improved; it can only be crucified. When we try to better ourselves, we miss the point. Only from the dust of a repentance to death will there be a possibility of resurrection. And only from a resurrected life will we ever know Him and be able to accomplish the works He has chosen for us and avoid those terrible words, "Go away from Me, I never knew you." The cross must be our source of life, even as it must be our source of death. And it must become our death before it becomes our life.

"Doing away with the cross" is anything less than the utter abandonment to Him of all that we are. It is anything less than a process of total death to self followed by resurrection life in His power.

If good messages and good music and good effort could do it, we wouldn't need the cross. But Jesus said that without Him, we can do nothing; and we continue to prove His words true when we try in our best intentions to do the work of the Kingdom and see our best efforts fall flat. When we allow the Holy Spirit to take over, He will take us to the cross before He takes us to the mission field, be it overseas or next door. At the end of the age, when we are brought face to face with the executioner's blade, it will not be a history of good messages and good music and good efforts that will set our faces like flint. It will only be because we have already died to this world and our very lives in it.

We have all been guilty, individually and otherwise, of doing away with the cross. May God have mercy on all of us that we may stand.

"Holy Spirit, we need Your revelation and leading and grace to rise to this call."

A Great Chasm

Due to sin, there is a great chasm between us and God. There is a narrow trail winding down one side of that chasm and up the other side. At the bottom is the cross. The only way to get there from here is to go down to the cross and pass through it. It is only there that we will find the atoning Blood of Jesus. Nothing that we can do or bring with us can be carried over unless it goes down and through the cross. No good idea of ours is of any value there. No good work of ours is of any value there. No motive or thought or breath of life counts for anything on the other side unless it has passed through the cross. Only what is done by Christ through us will last. Everything else will burn. No good deed or good intention will ever find its way to that other side unless it was Christ in us doing it. Our natural hearts are desperately wicked. We can conceive of and do no good thing of our own initiative. All of our motives are selfish and unclean, and we have nothing of value to offer — only ourselves as living sacrifices as we descend to the bottom and embrace the cross. Only then, in resurrection life and bearing the Lord's yoke, will we be able to produce lasting fruit. Anything less is a stench of self. To try to get from here to there, without going down and through the cross, is doing away with the cross.

FIFTEEN

Holiness and Victory

One evening several months ago the Holy Spirit seemed to say, "Without holiness there will be no victory." Prior to that I had been taken through two distinct occasions where the Lord showed me that my own impurity, in the form of thoughts and gazes that had not been taken captive, was a contributing cause of ministry failure as evidenced by the inability to overcome Satan. Where Satan is not overcome, the prisoners remain bound.

God continues to speak daily that without holiness, there will be no victory. He is saying, **"Be holy, for I am holy."** There is no acceptable alternative. We have been given everything we need to live holy lives by appropriating His precious promises. Ultimate victory at the end of the age will demand ultimate holiness, both individual and corporate. God is not planning to demonstrate His wisdom through a compromised Church mired in the clutches of sin, but through a holy and glorious Church. The extent of this goes beyond deed to include thought and glance and attitude, the hidden things of the innermost places. We should not try to justify anything less than perfection. God is probing into all areas of question in our lives and asking, "Would anything less be perfect?"

Seeing that His divine power has granted us **everything** pertaining to life and godliness, through the true knowledge of Him who called us by His own glory and excellence. For by these He has granted to us His precious and magnificent promises, in order that by them you might become **partakers of the divine nature, having escaped the corruption that is in the world by lust** (2 Peter 1:3-4).

When the Male Child Goes Up, Satan Comes Down

And she gave birth to a son, a male child, who is to rule all nations with a rod of iron; and her child was caught up to God and to His throne . . . And the great dragon was thrown down, the serpent of old who is called the devil and Satan, who deceives the whole world; he was thrown down to the earth, and his angels were thrown down with him. And I heard a loud voice in heaven, saying, "Now the salvation, and the power, and the kingdom of our God and the authority of His Christ have come, for the accuser of our brethren has been thrown down, who accuses them before our God day and night" (Revelation 12:5, 9-10).

When the male child of Revelation 12 is snatched up to heaven and to God's throne, Satan is thrown out of heaven to earth. It is no coincidence that these two events take place one after the other and in that order. God has elected to use His Church to defeat Satan, seemingly first by getting him thrown out of heaven to earth, and then by overcoming him on earth. It appears to be a two stage process. Remember, it was Satan falling from heaven to earth like lightning that Jesus envisioned after the victorious return of His seventy disciples. It was the result of this initial victory of His fledgling Church that prompted the vision of Satan's fall. The Bible says that after the appearance of the male child in heaven, "there was no longer a place for him [Satan] found in heaven." Michael and his angels do the actual fighting, but the fight seems predicated on the arrival in heaven of the first fruits of the harvest, the perfected male child for which all creation has been awaiting. Satan is displaced by the authority of the male child. And he is overcome on earth by a people who are victorious over him by the Blood of the Lamb, the word of their testimony, and by loving not their lives unto death. We can now begin to see why all creation is groaning for the revealing of the sons of God. It is the revealed sons of God who are given the authority of Jesus Christ to set all creation free from the bondage of Satan. Creation is not going to be restored until Satan is defeated, and the Church has the responsibility to carry out that defeat.

All Authority in Heaven and on Earth

> And Jesus came up and spoke to them, saying, **"All authority** has been given to Me in heaven and on earth (Matthew 28:18).

> And He said to them, "I was watching Satan fall from heaven like lightning. Behold, **I have given you authority** to tread upon serpents and scorpions, and over **all the power** of the enemy, and nothing shall injure you (Luke 10:18-19).

> And I also say to you that you are Peter, and upon this rock I will build My church; and the gates of Hades shall not overpower it. I will give you the keys of the kingdom of heaven; and **whatever you shall bind on earth shall be bound in heaven,** and whatever you shall loose on earth shall be loosed in heaven (Matthew 16:18-19).

All authority in heaven and on earth has been given to Jesus. And His disciples have in turn been given authority over **all** of the power of the enemy, **both** in heaven and on earth. What is bound on earth will be bound in heaven. All aspects of the victory over Satan which Jesus gained on the cross have been turned over to His Church for completion. Hence this victory in heaven over Satan has to await the maturity of the Church, and that maturity is first evidenced by the arrival of the perfected male child on the throne established and waiting for him from which to rule and reign.

The sequence is unmistakable. First comes holiness, then victory. It is the holy people of Daniel 12 whose power is shattered who are victorious and inherit the Kingdom. Our victory over Satan depends on our appropriating by faith all of the tools for godliness that God has provided for us through His precious and magnificent promises. Without faith, we will never believe God's promises and apply them to our sinful natures and situations. We will remain trapped in our sin, prisoners of the devil, and of no use in God's end-time purposes. We will be in danger of falling away, because Satan will have *something in us*, and with that hook he will reel us in.

Jesus died for us so that we could live pure and holy lives by escaping the corruption that is in the world. We are counseled to purge the leaven of sin from our lives and walk holy and blameless before Him. To the extent that we walk this out, we will escape the need to be purified during the fires of great tribulation. The sinners in the church at Thyatira were given time to repent, but they would not. Therefore, they were thrown into great tribulation. Those who seem to avoid great tribulation, and show up in heaven as first fruits of the harvest at the beginning of Revelation 14, are holy and blameless. They didn't start out holy. None of us do. But they have repented of their sins and allowed the cross to do a cleansing work in their lives. Satan has nothing in them. He has been displaced from their lives. There is no longer any place in them found for him. They have risen to that call to which each of us is called.

Obviously not every saint will qualify for the first-fruits harvest. It seems many of the Body of Christ will experience great tribulation to the extent necessary to be purified to the standard of the bride. There is leaven in our lives, which if not purged, will leaven the whole. We have not applied the tools of godliness to our lives in the form of the cleansing power of the cross to the degree that it was available.

There is no indication, however, that the two witnesses, or those in the church of Smyrna who are forewarned of imprisonment and death, are so destined because of sin in their lives. I think we have to be careful and not relate sinlessness or sinfulness to an exact destiny. We know that some in the church of Thyatira will be thrown into great tribulation because of their unwillingness to repent. However, the martyrs of Smyrna and the two witnesses are also on earth during this time. Remember, Jesus told Peter to follow Him and not worry about John. There is no indication that residual sin in Peter or Paul or Stephen was a direct cause of their martyrdoms. Certainly that was not the case with Jesus. Martyrdom is not a judgment; it is a crown of life. Some are destined to suffer because of sin; others are destined to suffer because of righteousness.

A Leaven Detector

One of the best ways to detect residual leaven in our lives is to look at our relationships with our brothers and sisters in the Body of Christ. We are to be living stones snugly fitted against the other living stones around us. Problems in relationships and discerning of the body indicate that there is leaven in our lives that must be purged. Paul said that because we do not properly discern the body, many of us are sick and some sleep. This is serious business. There is a clear warning and teaching here with application to our participation in the Lord's Supper. Our relationships with our brothers and sisters are a *litmus test* as to the condition of our spiritual walks. We can only relate to our brothers and sisters as Jesus lives through us to do so.

The Lord's Supper is an excellent time for reflection and repentance. **All** leaven must be purged. We can identify it now and take it to the cross, or it will be identified for us later amidst the fires of great tribulation. It's our choice. The words that Jesus speaks to each of us alive at the end of this age are, **"And all the Churches will know that I am He who searches minds and hearts and I will give to each of you according to your deeds."** All of us who consider ourselves

His disciples still have the option of deciding how we will finish this race. Will we embrace the cross now and be broken at its base, offering ourselves as living sacrifices and drink offerings to be poured out? Are we willing to let the alabaster flasks of our lives be broken and *wasted* on Jesus so that our testimonies can also be heard wherever the gospel is preached? Or are we practical and wise like Judas, concluding that the money could be better spent elsewhere?

There will be no anointing without holiness. Without anointing, there will be no ministry in the power and authority of Jesus. Without such ministry, there will be no setting of the captives free. There will be no victory over Satan who is keeping them bound. The gates of hell will not prevail over Jesus' Church. The gates of hell will prevail over those who are not holy and anointed in the power and authority of His name. The sons of Sceva will be prevailed over by the devil even though they mouth the name of Jesus and claim works in His name. "I recognize Jesus, and I know about Paul, but who are you?" The devil will know you when you have authority over him and his gates.

There is no place for leaven in such a war. There is no place for compromise. We either finish this race as winners or we lose and fall away. All of creation is awaiting our decision and the results of the race we will run. And Satan is awaiting our every flinch — our every drawing back, every chink in our armor. The deeper we go in the things of God, the greater is the surrounding pressure of the enemy trying to penetrate our shields. The closer to the front lines we choose to live — and it is a choice — the greater will be the firepower of the enemy. He will doggedly pursue us, picking away at our areas of weakness, bringing temptations into those areas in which we are most vulnerable. But God has given us the weapons to be victorious. Can we overcome the flesh and the devil by looking to Him for the victory?

Truth in the Innermost Parts

God is interested in truth in the innermost parts. I asked God several years back about a questionable area of conduct in my life and He replied, "Would anything less be perfect?" His standard is perfection, not achieved by self-generated discipline, but by the transformation and resulting life of the indwelling Spirit, without Whom we can do nothing. It is not that we become loving, or that we become holy, or that we become this or that. It is as He lives in us that His qualities emerge through us, and good fruit is borne.

"Seek first the Kingdom of God and His righteousness," Jesus said. There is an order here. There is no point in seeking righteousness until we have first sought the King. Righteousness is an outworking of our relationship with Jesus. He doesn't make us righteous; He is our righteousness. As we appropriate Him, we evidence His righteousness. It will save us a great deal of time if we set aside attempts to imitate His character and instead seek Him Who is the essence of that character. We don't need to be reformed; we need to die and be resurrected in the newness of His life. There is no place on the white wedding garment for spots caused by the flesh. **"By My Spirit,"** says the Lord. Watchman Nee refers to flesh buried shallow that still *stinks*. Our flesh must be buried so deep that no residual odor lingers. Our flesh has only one acceptable place and that is six feet down and dead. It may not stink to us because we have gotten used to it, but it is a stench to God. Flesh will not stand in His presence. Holy, Holy, Holy is the Lord God Almighty.

It is a holy people in the book of Daniel whose power is shattered and who receive the Kingdom for eternity. It is not a compromised, defeated people who fall away at the last minute. The two witnesses are not overcome because they fall into sin before the finish line. It is a victorious Army of God that walks to the cross, not a bunch of whimpering, defeated saints who trip and drop the baton on the last lap. These are holy and powerful and glorious saints who have the vision of Jesus before their eyes and who are marching in the ranks of His call. Remember, this is not about us but about Him. The appropriate sheep to be slaughtered is without blemish. These are those of whom the world is not worthy. The closer we rise to that standard by His grace, the more worthy we are as sacrifices for His end-time purposes. This is a holy calling for which His most precious saints are reserved. May we be found available, ready, and willing for this most honored of calls at the end of the age. Many are answering it today. Many are the ranks who have already answered it and found their way to eternal glory. But, unfortunately, many are those who will fall away.

"Lord, help us to rise to this call. Help us. Give us the strength to stand before kings and governors and testify of You. Let it be our testimony that overcomes the evil one and sends the gospel to the ends of the earth."

The Fuel to Endure

Are we passionate about this pursuit of holiness? Without passion, we will just be trying to do a job, and we will fail. It is our love for Him that must fuel us. And we love Him because He first loved us. If we do not have a revelation of His fiery love for us, we will not be able to embrace the cross in the fullness required. We will not fully understand that God disciplines only those He loves. It is for noble or ignoble purposes that we are at this time being shaped on the potter's wheel. What is our choice?

God's passion and jealousy burn for us like a jealous lover. His hot love is the substance from which passion is modeled between a husband and a wife. When we look with lust at *another thing*, be it another person or an idol, we break His heart, for He is jealous for our single-eyed affection. He is jealous for our time, for our silence before Him in waiting, for our hunger for His whisper. He calls us to the secret place behind closed doors, the place where lovers go. He woos us with quiet whispers and intimations, but we are often focused on other things. Still He comes, patiently, softly knocking.

We must see that the events touching us to transform us are a result of God's passion for us, not just ordinary love, but passion! We must understand this when we go into the lion's den or the fiery furnace or the prison or the hospital bed. We must lay down our lives with the full knowledge of, and direct consequence of, God's passion for us. "God must hate me because He is allowing this" has no place in our outlook. God disciplines **only** those He loves. God allows these things into our lives to purify us for an eternal weight of glory in His Kingdom.

> Women received back their dead by resurrection; and others were tortured, not accepting their release, in order that they might obtain a better resurrection; and others experienced mockings and scourgings, yes, also chains and imprisonment. They were stoned, they were sawn in two, they were tempted, they were put to death with the sword; they went about in sheepskins, in goatskins, being destitute, afflicted, ill-treated (men of whom the world was not worthy), wandering in deserts and mountains and caves and holes in the ground. And all these, having gained approval through their faith, did not receive what was promised, because God had provided something better for us, so that apart from us they should not be made perfect.

> Therefore, since we have so great a cloud of witnesses surrounding us, let us also lay aside every encumbrance, and the sin which so easily entangles us, and let us run with endurance the race that is set before us, fixing our eyes on Jesus, the author and perfecter of faith, who for the joy set before Him endured the cross, despising the shame, and has sat down at the right hand of the throne of God. For consider Him who has endured such hostility by sinners against Himself, so that you may not grow weary and lose heart. You have not yet resisted to the point of shedding blood in your striving against sin; and you have forgotten the exhortation which is addressed to you as sons, "My son, do not regard lightly the discipline of the Lord, nor faint when you are reproved by Him; for those whom the Lord loves He disciplines, and He scourges every son whom He receives." It is for discipline that you endure; God deals with you as with sons; for what son is there whom his father does not discipline? But if you are without discipline, of which all have

become partakers, then you are illegitimate children and not sons (Hebrews 11:35-12:8).

Suffering and Holiness and Salvation

For the last three years the Lord has allowed something very remarkable to happen on my birthday. The first time it happened, I was shattered. I thought to myself, "What kind of birthday present is this?" I have had the joy and privilege in the last three years to lead three people to the Lord. These are the only three people to date that I have actually led to the Lord. All three accepted Jesus as their personal Lord and Savior. All three were terminally ill patients — two with advanced cancer and one a stroke victim. All three faded away over a long process of gradual deterioration. All three suffered. All three, one each year, died early on the morning of my birthday, April 21. Lilia died in 1997, Harry in 1998, and Francis in 1999. During those three years, the Lord was taking me through a teaching on the redemptiveness of suffering out of which came Chapter Six of this book.

When I visited Francis for the last time on April 20, 1999, his blood pressure was down to below fifty and dropping. He was suffering, but I could not grieve for him, because he had come to Jesus for salvation and had received it. God's fiery passion was brooding over him bringing forth eternal life as he lay there in that hospital bed with tubes running in and out of him. I felt led to bend over and whisper in his ear that angels might come to visit him that night and that it was okay to go with them. Sometime early the next morning they came and took him.

He had suffered, but his suffering was redemptive because it had brought him to the place where he had set aside his resistance and bitterness and received Jesus Christ as his Lord and Savior. He continued to suffer after that decision up until the day the Lord took him. Perhaps he was being purified during this time. Perhaps he was filling up his quota of additional suffering allotted to the Body of Christ. For whatever reason, God let him suffer as a member of the

Body of Christ until the morning the angels came and took him.

After going through this identical scenario three years in a row, I have lost most of my fear of death. Death is a defeated foe. I have lost most of my confusion over suffering, which might otherwise seem needless and cruel. When I was born in 1946, April 21 was Easter Sunday, resurrection morning. I know the Lord is speaking of salvation and resurrection and eternal life in all of this. Suffering for the King is glorious and life-giving. Francis and Harry and Lilia know that now. Let the testimonies of their suffering be an encouragement to all of us. They have paid a price to demonstrate this lesson for our instruction.

> For it was fitting for Him, for whom are all things, and through whom are all things, in bringing many sons to glory, to perfect the author of their salvation through sufferings. For both He who sanctifies and those who are sanctified are all from one Father; for which reason He is not ashamed to call them brethren (Hebrews 2:10-11).

It is going to be His Body, perfected through suffering, that fulfills the call at the end of this age to lay down their lives for His redemptive purposes. How could it be otherwise? We are called to follow Him.

Song to the Bride

Only the glance and woo of a lover can draw the bride to the heights that she is destined to skip freely on. And it is on such heights where He dwells. It is there where He dwells that we are called. "Come, My precious bride, come up higher. Let the fiery passion of My glance wake you from your bed of slumber to seek Me on the heights. It is as you seek Me that you will find Me. I am constrained to remain hidden if you will not seek Me. It is your very unrest that reveals your spirit crying out for Me. I made your spirit that way. It can be satisfied with no other lover, because your spirit is pure. It is only Myself that I have made you hunger for, though you may not know it. Your longing cannot be fulfilled by all of the pleasure, power, and wealth the world has to offer. You have chased all of that and not found the satisfaction that you long for. Not if you had all of it would you be satisfied. I know. Solomon knows. Because I have made you to be unsatisfied with any or all of that. All the longings of your heart are designed to bring you home to Me. Why do you seek so many distractions and side trips on the way? The intimacy of a wife and husband are only a shadow of the intimacy I desire with you. I have had to dilute My passion for you to represent a shadow of it in the intimacy of first love on earth between a maid and her lover. But this is only a shadow. You may not understand this because you can only relate to passion on earth, because you have no other comparison. Do you want a comparison? Do you want to know the real thing? Here I am. I stand at the door and knock. You may be a prodigal, but I am the Father of prodigals, and I am waiting to run and meet you when I see you coming. I will put a ring on your finger, a robe on your shoulders, and we will celebrate! When My Son taught the parable of the prodigal, He was revealing My heart toward you as your Father."

"Father, we do not see these things as we ought to see them. Open our eyes, Father, and give us visions of glory, of eternal things. Give us the precious gift of revelation concerning how much You love us, how passionate You are to dwell in and possess the innermost parts of who we are. Father, Your ways are above and beyond us. Our thoughts are not Your thoughts. We rely on You to bring us into the understanding and the fullness of these things for You have chosen us since before time began to be conformed to the likeness of Your Son. Thank You for this gift that is beyond our ability to measure or comprehend or express the wealth of. And when our time comes, with Your grace, we pray that we might stand and set our faces like flint to endure for our sakes and for Your glory.

"Father, perfect us through the crucible fires of Your passionate love and mercy and then slay us on Your altar for Your glory and Your glory alone. Only in this way will we achieve the eternal joy for which we are designed and long. We ask this in Jesus' name. May it be so."

The Morning Star

> Arise, shine; for your light has come, and the glory of the LORD has risen upon you. For behold, darkness will cover the earth, and deep darkness the peoples; but the LORD will rise upon you, and His glory will appear upon you. And nations will come to your light, and kings to the brightness of your rising (Isaiah 60:1-3).

> And he who overcomes, and he who keeps My deeds until the end, TO HIM I WILL GIVE AUTHORITY OVER THE NATIONS; AND HE SHALL RULE THEM WITH A ROD OF IRON, AS THE VESSELS OF THE POTTER ARE BROKEN TO PIECES, as I also have received authority from My Father; and I will give him the morning star (Revelation 2:26-28).

The overcomers in the church at Thyatira (as opposed to those of the church at Thyatira who are thrown into great tribulation) are promised to rule and reign as well as be given the morning star. The morning star becomes visible in the heavens before the sun comes up. It is actually not a star, but a planet reflecting the light of the sun. It is a precursor of the sun, an announcer of its soon coming. It is the sign that night is almost over and that dawn is about to break. It may be a picture of the first fruits of the main harvest who are snatched to the throne of God from which to rule and reign. Their first job upon arrival will be to boot Satan out of heaven to earth. Those of us still on earth will crush him underfoot by the wisdom of the cross. He's on his way to the fires of hell. Don't let him convince you otherwise and don't let him drag you with him.

A Closing Prayer

"Father, we praise You for the incompetence of the flesh that You allow us to demonstrate that drives us to You in poverty of spirit, bankrupt of all anointing. Thank You, Father, that in many things we were not overnight successes, but rather overnight failures. Thank You for Your grace. By the very nature of the failures that You have allowed us to walk through, You have demonstrated Your love for us, in that to think that without You we can do anything is a deception of grave peril. Thank You for Your chastenings, Father. By them we are identified as sons. Truly we see that we have reason to rejoice in all things, even in our shortcomings, for out of them You create blessing in order to make all things work for our good. Please continue to refine us, Father, so that we may become worthy vessels to contain Your glory at the end of the age. Transform us into those of the bride company without spot or wrinkle. No one comes to You unless drawn, Father, and we pray that You would prompt us to seasons of dedicated prayer and seeking so that we can be ambassadors of the Kingdom and not betrayers.

"Heavenly Father, may these words glorify You and present this teaching as I believe Your Holy Spirit has given it. If these words are a helpful teaching of Your plan for the destiny of Your Church, may they be fruitful and find audience as You see fit. May they bring forth much fruit to Your glory. Otherwise, may they come to nothing, and may You have mercy on this poor teacher.

"Heavenly Father, we praise You for Your master plan which is far beyond our ability to understand. Through us, Your Church, You have said that You will demonstrate Your wisdom to the rulers and authorities in the heavenly places. Give us Your Spirit of wisdom and revelation to properly discern truth from deception in these matters and to understand the nature and importance of this call.

"In the authority and power and in the name of Jesus, I pray to bind the efforts of the enemy to establish and maintain deception in this critical area of our knowledge and vision. I pray to bind his efforts to trap the Church with deceptive and misleading doctrine concerning the course of end-time events, those events of which You have warned us in advance so that we would specifically not be deceived. I pray to break the power of the enemy presently blinding the eyes of the Church to Your clear teachings. I pray to loose a spirit of wisdom and revelation upon a sleeping Church.

"Father, we seek Your mercy, grace, wisdom, and revelation so that we do not fall away in these upcoming times due to any deception the enemy has sown. We pray that our love may not grow cold due to the increasing lawlessness around us. May You grant us Your grace and strength to stand before You in these times, and may we be found worthy of the Kingdom. May we, if appropriate, be found worthy to be kept from the hour of testing at the end of the age granted to the overcomers of the church of Philadelphia and as described in Luke 21:36.

"May we learn to seek only You and Your direction for our lives. May we all be brought to full stature through the purifying crucible of the times before us as required. Father, we desire to walk before You in the power and authority of Your Son. Embolden us and strengthen us and be for us the source of all things, for without You we can do nothing. We strip ourselves empty and bare before You for this purpose. We lay all things on the altar which would interfere with Your eternal plan. We offer ourselves as living sacrifices. Lord Jesus, create in us such burning passion that we have no other thought than to follow You wherever You go. May Your passionate prayer of John 17 be fulfilled within us. Give us the grace of the strength of the joy of bridal love without which we would surely fall away.

"We say 'Yes, Lord!' to each of our individual and corporate destinies that will one day realize the fulfillment of Your plan and the transformation of each of us into Your likeness. We desire to enlist in Your army with You as our Commander-in-Chief. May all glory and honor and praise in these things be eternally Yours. May we, by Your grace, allow the demonstration of Your wisdom through us, and we praise You and thank You for such honor and privilege. May we please You in our service. May we all overcome and hear those joyous words, 'Well done good and faithful servants!' Praise and glory and honor to You, Father, for the gift of Your

Son and for the transformations He is working within each of us to conform us to His likeness and bring us to Your ultimate destiny for each of us. Let nothing prevent us from reaching those final ultimate destinies. Let us all finish the race well. Father, we, like Paul, want to know Jesus and the power of His resurrection and the fellowship of His sufferings.

"In trust of Your everlasting mercy and grace to those who call upon Your name, we lay these things before You and await the glorious return of Your Son to rescue us, to transform us, and to transport us into Your glorious presence. May You come quickly, Lord Jesus!! **The Spirit and the bride say, 'Come, Lord Jesus!' Amen."**

Preparing the Way Publishers

makes available practical materials
(books, booklets, and audio tapes)
that call the Church to the radical Christianity
described in the Bible.

Some titles include —
The Way to God
Basic Bible Studies
Getting to Know GOD
New Testament Survey Course
Mastering the Word of God – and Letting it Master You
You Can be a Soul Winner – Here's How!
The Church Triumphant at the End of the Age
New Wine Skins – the Church in Transition
God's Simple Plan for His Church – a Manual for House Churches
Leadership–Servanthood in the Church as found in the New Testament
Woman – God's Plan not Man's Tradition
Restoring the Vision of the End-times Church

For further information, see the PTW web page
at http://www.PTWPublish.com

For a free catalog and order form contact —

Preparing the Way Publishers
2121 Barnes Avenue SE
Salem, OR 97306, USA

phone 503/585-4054
fax 503/375-8401
e-mail kruppnj@open.org

Printed in the United States
80271LV00002B/68